Encompassed Purpose

Action & Purpose

Author
Bradley Berg

34. Do your best, but do something
35. Live life as a beginner
36. Learn from others – learn, learn, learn
37. Positive mental manifestation
38. Gratitude
39. Give
40. Kick butt!
41. Action
42. Embrace your new you
43. Listen to the inner voice
44. Beliefs
45. Higher power
46. Courage
47. Discipline – performance – goals
48. Gut instinct
49. Leadership and servitude
50. Destiny, dreams and pathway
51. Coach, mentor, consultants
52. Don't do it alone
53. Balance your life
54. Encompassed goals
55. Encompassed purpose
56. Act

ISBN: 978-057860607-1 (Paperback)

Library of Congress Control Number: Pending
ISSN : Pending

Any references to historical events, real people, or real
places
are used fictitiously. Names, characters and places are
products of the author's imagination.

Printed by
First printing edition 2019.

Encompassed Purpose/B.C.C.
835 Hwy 42 Po Box 337
Iberia, Missouri 65486

www.encompassedpurpose.com

Dedication

This is written for every person and organization so you can take control over your actions and goals to achieve an accountable purposeful existence.

2 Corinthians 6:11-13 The Message (MSG)

11-13 Dear Corinthians, I can't tell you how much I long for you to enter this wide-open, spacious life. We didn't fence you in. The smallness you feel comes from within you. Your lives aren't small, but you're living them in a small way. I'm speaking as plainly as I can, and with great affection. Open up your lives. Live openly and expansively!

Acknowledgment

I want to thank Timothy Flora & Shelby Berg for editing and deciphering my words and ideas, and Kim Wennerlyn for the cover design.

Overview

When I decided to write this book, it was not for the reasons most do. I decided, after decades of reading, programs, etc., it needed to be done. There are items intentionally left out of self-help, motivational and business books because it hinders book sales. But leaving that information out will also hinder true growth and development in you.

It hinders substantial, long-lasting, sustainable improvements in your life, business and family. I wrote this with one intention - to help people - and if it helps one person or a million people, I have succeeded. This is not a long book, so It's a quick read that you can go back and reference many times.

This is a no holds-barred way for you to empower and evolve. It includes some difficult things if done properly, but the reward is so large and abundant that the journey is well with it.

This book was designed for one purpose - to help you and give a clear understanding of how to do it. It may not make this book the most popular, but it will make it the most effective for a happy, fulfilled, peaceful life or business.

Many times in this book you will see me to refer to life or business. There are multiple reasons for this. The methods are the same, whether you realize it or not. And for many of the small business owners I work with, their businesses are very important and intertwined in their life. If you don't have a business, no worries, because you do have a life and a career. Substitute the word business with career, and don't make an excuse why you can't do this.

Most importantly, this book has real truths about the Trinity and the Bible, and you will see most every self-help, motivational and development book has gotten its inspiration from that once source, the Bible.

When you are done with this book you can have an encompassed purpose and live a fulfilled, happy, accountable life. Stop being a victim, stop being negative and coming up with every excuse why you are not where you want to be. You are not where you want to be because of you, or because you did not have the knowledge and tools to fix that. Well you now begin your journey. You have in your hand what can start you on your way to live your destiny. Take the first step and get the book. Read the book, then go back and do the steps and processes. Go back and reference when you are lost. But start today. You can begin to change your life today.

Life

It's funny how much we complicate what was so easy. You were born carefree and happy, and that carries on.

Have you ever noticed toddlers? They waddle around smiling not caring what they're wearing. They don't care about the latest and greatest. They walk around with their belly hanging out, laughing at everything and smiling. We need to be more like that again. Well maybe no belly hanging out. I guess that's a personal choice.

You ever watch a toddler waddle too quickly and fall down? They either get right back up, or if they really wiped out, they may cry for mere seconds then are off and running again.

They don't dwell on it, thinking "Oh gosh, if I run again I may fall again." No, they take off and enjoy life. They are too happy with life to realize they will fall, and even when they get a little older they know they will fall again but would rather live life and accept falling as a fact. They realize they are going to fall and it's okay. They have done it before, and when it happens they get back up and start playing again.

They don't dwell on what happened the last time. They don't have fear or worry. Somehow many adults have lost this and say "well, I will just sit here, because if I stand up again I may fall."

Toddlers don't hold onto grudges about the floor for years. They know it's not the floor, it could have been many things, including them tripping themselves up, which adults do a lot through self-sabotage. They get back up and go again.

So what happened? How did we get to where every fall, every little ant hill turns into a mountain? Why are we so paralyzed by failure and what others think that we stop living life, and fall into a random existence in a fog, like we have no control? I am here to tell you do have control of your life. You also have guidance.

Ecclesiastes 1:12-15 NIV "What is twisted cannot be straightened" refers to the ultimate perplexity and confusion that comes to us because of all the unanswered questions in life. Solomon, writing about his own life, discovered that neither his accomplishments nor his wisdom could make him truly happy. True wisdom is found in God, and true happiness comes from pleasing him.

You were born

When you were born you have predetermined influences, your family, no matter what that looks like, had beliefs before you were born. They accepted their beliefs as their own, then you were indoctrinated from day one. Before you could even comprehend what they were saying their beliefs were being instilled in you.

From the first moment of understanding you were told exactly what to think and how to act, whether that is educated or street wise, rich or poor, positive or negative, thrill seeker or fearful. While everyone has certain personality traits of their own, most of us had a predetermined belief cycle in planted in us from day one.

You are taught by the influences around you how to talk, carry yourself, your mindset, beliefs, economic status, modest or flashy, money is important or money is the root of all evil. I could go on, but you get the picture.

2 Timothy 2:22-26
22 Flee the evil desires of youth and pursue righteousness, faith, love and peace, along with those who call on the Lord out of a pure heart. 23 Don't have anything to do with foolish and stupid arguments, because you know they produce quarrels. 24 And the Lord's servant must not be quarrelsome but must be kind to everyone, able to

teach, not resentful. 25 Opponents must be gently instructed, in the hope that God will grant them repentance leading them to a knowledge of the truth, 26 and that they will come to their senses and escape from the trap of the devil, who has taken them captive to do his will.

As you start to grow throw you childhood you surround yourself in many cases with like-minded people. That carries throughout adulthood. Because of our beliefs we surround ourselves with people that confirm and support our beliefs and stay in the bubble of comfort, or in many cases misery, until now.

Now for the good news that you can change anytime you want. There are some hard truths you are going to have to accept along the way, but if you really want to be better in all aspects of life and business, some of the uncomfortable things, and things that will be hard to swallow, will be very worth it for the kind of fulfillment you can and should have.

Many of you will have trouble accepting this at first, but most of you are where you are today because of your beliefs, your thought process, mindset and behaviors.

Proverbs10:2 NIV Some people bring unhappiness on themselves by choosing ill-gotten treasures. For example, craving satisfaction, they may do something that destroys their chances of ever achieving happiness. God's principles for right living bring lasting happiness because they guide us into long-term right behavior in spite of our ever-changing feelings.

Your conscious and subconscious thoughts have been instilled in your life today. Don't live your life on the illusions of someone else's beliefs. If you are reading this, you are wise enough and interested enough to have your own belief system. If you have an underlying thought, conscious or subconscious, it's not as easy as saying change your mindset, or do this and you will be fixed.

We will look at underlying beliefs, guilt, burden and self-sabotage, and how to correct it and live the life and have the business you dreamed of, not the life and business you dreaded.

I am not saying throw out your belief system. All I am saying is you have evolved and expanded from your limiting beliefs to a more powerful belief system. Take away your narrow view, take the padlock off your brain and open it up.

Expand, evolve and learn you have spectacular opportunities. So drop your ego, let your guarded walls of set in your way beliefs down, and evolve your mind from limiting beliefs to the life you deserve with limitless possibilities.

Proverbs 1:7-9 NIV In this age of information, knowledge is plentiful, but wisdom is scarce. Wisdom means far more than simply knowing. A lot it is a basic attitude that affects every aspect of your life. The foundation of knowledge is to fear the Lord - to honor and respect him, to live in awe of his power and obey his Word. Faith in God - he will make you truly wise.

Self-evaluation and reflection

I debated where to put this because it's tough, but I thought this is the proper place because once you do this, you will have a huge weight lifted from you. This is just one part of self-evaluation and reflection, but it's substantial, and if you can do this, and truly do it this, it will be the most wonderful yet possibly the hardest things you have ever done.

Galatians 6:4-5 NIV Each one should test his own actions. Then he can take pride in himself, without comparing himself to somebody else, 5. for each should carry his own load.
6:4 When you do your very best, you feel good about the results. There is no need to compare yourself with others. People make comparisons for many reasons. Some point out others' flaws in order to feel better about themselves. Others simply want reassurance there are doing well. When we are tempted to compare, look at Jesus Christ. His example will inspire you to do your very best, and his loving acceptance will comfort you when you fall short of your expectations.

Self-evaluation has many parts to it. There are many upcoming pages and chapters that are part of the encompassing self-evaluation process. I recommend reading through the entire book so you can complete the full process, then coming back and starting this full process again, or you are not going to do yourself justice with what this can truly do for you. If you truly follow this and the following chapters, it will be one of the most powerful, uplifting experiences you have ever done.

The problem is the half-washed idea of it. If it is not difficult, then you are not all in. You're glazing over what will truly help you. Go all in, release the baggage and burdens, and be up lifted like never before.

Now is where I will lose some of you who are not ready to improve. Some will do it halfway, some will say I am out, but others will embrace it with their whole heart and take it on.

So what is it?

There are many chapters to follow that are self-evaluation and reflection, however I felt this needed to be on its own. The first time you do this it should be substantial. Then I would recommend it on a daily basis. Take a time out and pause to reflect every day.

What did I do well?

What could I do better?

What would I change?

What is not where I am looking to go?

What have I improved upon?

What were time wasters or busy work?

What brought me closer to my dreams?

What strengthened my spirituality?
What brought me closer to my goals, dreams and vision?
What helped me align, brought clarity and furthered my path?   This is such a powerful tool and can help your growth so much if you allow it to. This is just an example. You can add, subtract and change it to fit your life and business. It depends on the areas you need to work on and the areas you do well.

Take the major arguments, major hurts, major setbacks. Now if you think they are an evil person, business, organization or group, take them out of the equation so you just have the situation. Don't justify your actions, or you will be doing this wrong.

When have you had arguments, hurts, setbacks, used people, taken advantage of people or entities or have wronged others in any way? You know you have, and you know which ones the most. You carry with you that baggage and waste your time on recurring thoughts. Be honest with yourself and really give it thought.

Corinthians 13:3-7 NIV If I give all I possess to the poor and surrender my body to the flames, but have not love, I gain nothing. 4 Love is patient, love is kind. It does not envy, it does not boast, it is not proud. 5 It is not rude, it is not self-seeking, it is not easily angered, it keeps no record of wrongs. 6. Love does not rejoice in evil, but rejoices with

the truth. 7. It always protects, always trusts,
always hopes, always perseveres.
13. 4-7 Our society confuses love and lust. Unlike
lust, God's kind of love is directed outwards
towards others, not inward toward ourself. It is is
utterly unselfish. This kind of love goes against our
natural inclinations. It is possible to practice this
love only if God helps us set aside our own desires
and instincts, so we can give love, while expecting
nothing in return. Thus, the more we become like
Christ, the more love we will show to others.

It doesn't matter what they did to you. Take the person, group or entity entirely out of the equation. You have to take responsibility for your life. You can totally change your life and it doesn't matter what your parents did or didn't do, what the company did, what a past relationship did, etc. Keep reading and you will see why.

No one can make you feel any way. You choose anger, sadness, hurt, happiness, fulfillment and joy. Many people go through life without stopping to do self-reflection and assessing their life, their responsibility and accountability.

One person comes to mind. She was very intelligent but did terrible things. However, if someone did one little thing to her it was blown up from an ant hill to a mountain. She would blame all her life issues on others and embellished as she went along. She moved around the country with many failed relationships and many failed marriages by age 30. Always seeking more, she was never satisfied or really experienced fulfilled happiness long-term.

She always played the role of the victim, and no matter what had actually happened it was always someone else's fault. Even when no one else but her made the choice, she could manipulate, twist and somehow find a way to claim it was someone else. She always wondered why she was unhappy, angry, stressed and unfulfilled. She moved and made up her version of the truth for people until she believed it.

You can do anything you want as long as you are willing to suffer the consequences of your actions. Her life was reduced to the existence above because of her actions. The truth is the person had many wonderful opportunities for her life. The only thing that made her life terrible instead of her dream, was her mindset.

Do you know people like this? Are you like this? You do not have to wait one more day to start living a wonderful life. You will never do that fully until you self-reflect, take responsibility and accountability for your life.

Matthew 7:1-5 NIV Do not judge or you to will be judged 2. For the same way you judge others, you will be judged, and with the measure you use, it will be measured. 3. Why do you look at the speck of sawdust in your brother's eye and pay no attention to the plank in your own eye? 4. How can

*you say to your brother, let me take the speck out
of your eye, when all the time there is a plank in
your eye? 5. You hypocrite, first take the plank out
of your own eye, then you will see clearly to
remove the speck from your own eye.*
*7:1,2 Jesus tells us to examine our own motives
and conduct instead of judging others. The traits
that bother us in others are often the habits we
dislike in ourselves. Our untamed bad habits and
behavior patterns are the very ones we most want
to change in others. Do you find it easy to magnify
others' faults while excusing your own? If you are
ready to criticize someone, check to see if you
deserve the same criticism. Judge yourself first,
then lovingly forgive and help your neighbor.*
*7:1-5 Jesus statement "do not judge" is against
the hypocritical, judgmental attitude that tears
others down in order to build oneself up. It's not a
blanket statement against all critical thinking, but
a call to discernment rather than negativity.*

Set it in motion and take action. Do what is needed
and discipline yourself for what you want to be
and what you want to do.

It's time for you to take charge of your life
and stop blaming, making excuses or playing the
role of the victim. You need to self-examine your
life to live it to the fullest extent. You are capable
of so much if you allow yourself to be.

Work through your misalignments, values,
behaviors and goals. If it is not getting you where

you want to be, why are you wasting your time doing it. Let resentment, anger and the past in general go. The only one you are hurting is you. Focus on what you want - your dreams, goals and purpose.

If what you did was wrong, own it. How could you have handled it differently? How could you have taken the higher ground? Reflect on how and what you did, and how that may have affected the person, group or entity. Really give deep thought to the many situations throughout your life.

You may have had setbacks and hardships beyond your control, but that does not mean you stay there. That is where this chapter and the upcoming chapters come in to play. Stop kicking the can and start kicking butt.

Haggai 1:5-7 NIV Now this is what the Lord Almighty says: Give careful thoughts to your ways. You have planted much, but you harvested little. You eat, but you never have enough. You drink, but you never have your fill. You put on clothes, but are not warm. You earn wages, only to put them in a purse with holes in it. 7. This is what the Lord Almighty says: Give careful thought to your ways. 1:3-6 God asked his people how they could live in luxury when his house was lying in ruins. The temple was the focal point of Judah's relationship with God, but still it was demolished. Instead of rebuilding the temple, the people put their energies into beautifying their own homes. However, the harder the people worked for themselves, the less they had because they ignored their spiritual lives. The same happens with us. If we put God first, he will provide for our deepest needs. If we put him in any other place, all our efforts will be futile. Caring only for your physical needs while ignoring your relationship to God will lead to ruin.

Where are your priorities? Where is your lifestyle? How do you treat people - all people. Reflect and reach into your past, including memories you have suppressed, twisted or manipulated and really think about it.

Be honest with yourself. Because until you are, you are stuck with what you have. If it angers you or upsets you too much, read on and come back to it when you are ready. But it's a must. List it, or them, here.

If you're 30 and have 10 things listed you did not do this right. Ten things really? This is to help you so do not cheat yourself. You may be upset, angry or hurt right now, but trust me on this, if you cheat this process you are cheating yourself. If you need additional paper, grab a note pad write it all down.

If you took this seriously, congratulations. You have taken a big step towards improving your life. Take a deep breath and let's begin to fix it. In the following pages you will be able to let go of the heaviness and baggage and begin to start letting go of everything.

How can I align myself for where I want to go and what I want to do and be?

What am I doing that is not aligned with what I want?

What will I stop to improve my life?

What is my busy work I should stop?

What are my time wasters I should stop?

In what areas will I increase my responsibility and accountability?

In what areas will I work on daily to improve myself?

How can I align my walk with God?

How can I make my life more fulfilled?

How can I be content?

How can I be happier and more joyful?

If you do not know, come back to it. Keep reading

and you will. We will be covering this throughout the book, but this is very important. I know it can be hard to swallow, but if you practice the self-reflection techniques throughout this book you will see how wonderful it can be. Feel free to come back if it is too much at once. There is no hurry and it's better to take your time.

Forgive and ask for forgiveness

Okay, my recommendation now is to first ask for forgiveness. There is no right or wrong way to do this, as long as your heart and mind are in the right place.

Romans 12:17-21 NIV Do not repay anyone evil for evil. Be careful to do what is right in the eyes of everybody. 18 If it is possible, as far as it depends on you, live at peace with everyone. 19. Do not take revenge, I will repay, says the Lord. 20 On the contrary: "If your enemy is hungry, feed him; if he is thirsty, give him something to drink. In doing this, you will heap burning coals on his head. 21. Do not be overcome by evil, but overcome evil with good.
12:17-21 These verses summarize Christian living. If we love someone the way Christ loves us, we will be willing to forgive. If we have experienced God's grace, we will want to pass it on to others. And remember, we're not excusing misdeeds. We're recognizing him, forgiving him, and loving him in spite of his sins - just as Christ did for us.

I want to say first if there is a situation you are going to ask forgiveness for that may put you in danger or harm your life in any way, or if you have exhausted efforts to find the person or whatever it might be, then do the following.

Write a letter. Please put everything in this

letter so it's sincere and you can have closure. Okay, do you feel you properly asked for forgiveness? If so, take the letter and burn it or throw it in the trash.

Now don't use the above for a scapegoat. This is only for cases of danger or harm. For the rest of the situations, in person, letter, text, phone call, whatever is possible. That does not mean take the most comfortable way for you. Do what is proper and must be done.

That being said, there are also baby steps. Maybe a letter is all the courage you can muster for now. That is okay. Maybe later in your journey you will call or meet, but you took a big step, and if you truly poured your heart and soul into it ,you will have closure for what you have done.

It does not matter what happened to you. We will get to that later. This is what you did and about you. It does not matter if the person accepts your apology or responds, or how they react you cannot control that and you have, with all your heart and soul, asked for forgiveness. Does it feel a wrecking ball has been lifted off your chest? Does it feel as if your brain is less cluttered and has more clarity? It should if you were true to yourself.

Note: During this process it won't be an hour long or day event. As it occurs in your mind you will have your large group of first thoughts, then two things will happen. Others will trickle in and with the first group you will remember additional things that you are now ready to tell yourself. The truth about that may require an additional apology.

I would highly recommend not overwhelming yourself with this. The most important part of this process is the sincerity, not the speed. Take your time, over a month or two if you need it. It's not easy and needs to be thought out and thoughtful. **Please do not do this until you have read the following.**

Forgiveness

I will tell from experience you can't truly forgive until you do what is needed, which is almost all the time you ask for forgiveness for what you have done. It's human nature to blame and ignore what we have done. This can be personally, or in the business world. It doesn't matter, but it's time to start a new chapter.

There are many reasons for that. If you forgive without asking for forgiveness first, no matter what the situation was you're the bad guy. Now others don't say that because it's easy to say yeah, I will forgive that person, and I am the better person.

While that may temporarily work, it will dawn on you, being the brilliant person you are, that it all can't be forgiven until you ask for forgiveness, because you are not acknowledging the whole truth.

Maybe Bob punched you in the nose in front of your friends, so why should you apologize to him? Well you did take Bob's biggest customer and devastated his company.

Maybe your spouse cheated on you. That's his or her issue, but you can apologize for other issues in the marriage, or the way you reacted.

You see, at this point it's not about forgiving them. It's about saying if I am the absolute best I can be I have still done wrong, and can admit that. Is that why your spouse cheated?

Absolutely not. Did you ever do any wrong in your marriage? Of course you did. And you can acknowledge that.

Example: I did not know better then, but I did _____. I am working at being the best person I can be and I apologize for not taking the initiative back then to know what I know now. And it is important to me to tell you that I now know I could have done better with_____, _____, _____. I hope you accept my apology and hope for the best for your future.

It can be that simple and their reaction does not matter. Then let it go drop it from your memory and release the burden you have been carrying around.

You see, you are accomplishing many things. You are acknowledging your shortcomings and know that because you are becoming a better person.

You are asking for forgiveness for many reasons.

1. you could have done better.
2. so the person you are asking forgiveness from knows you acknowledge mistakes and it's up to them how they react to it. Even though you might not see it, you made an impact in a positive way for them.
3. You are able to forgive yourself for what you have done, consciously or subconsciously, and

release the burden from your life.

Lastly, maybe someone did something terrible to you and you did nothing at all to deserve it. The fact you are still holding onto it is giving them power. You have the power, and it's time you take control and decide enough is enough. That toxic person or situation no longer deserves a part in your thoughts.

Forgiving – Part 2

Not forgiving someone is toxic for you, not them. I have seen this example many times, but it's like you taking poison and and waiting for your enemy to die. In many cases, the person you are angry or upset with, hurt by, or hold a grudge against does not care, or has no idea and is living their life. While in your mind, when you think of that person or situation, you take another spoonful of poison and swallow the bitterness.

2 Corinthians 7:2-7

2 Make room for us in your hearts. We have wronged no one, we have corrupted no one, we have exploited no one. 3 I do not say this to condemn you; I have said before that you have such a place in our hearts that we would live or die with you. 4 I have spoken to you with great frankness; I take great pride in you. I am greatly encouraged; in all our troubles, my joy knows no bounds. 5 For when we came into Macedonia, we had no rest. But we were harassed at every turn - conflicts on the outside, fears within. 6 But God, who comforts the downcast, comforted us by the coming of Titus. 7 and not only by his coming but also by the comfort you had given him. He told us about your longing for me, your deep sorrow, your ardent concern for me, so that my joy was greater than ever.

Now you may say forgiving can be a hard thing. You may say I forgave_____, but in your mind it comes up from time to time. Then you have not forgiven _____. I know, I know, I forgave but I don't forget. BULL!

You can forgive and remember, but it's a totally different feeling. This process is easier than asking for forgiveness. Why would you want the person that hurt you to have control over your life?

If you still have bitterness, resentment, anger, or hurt, or feel wronged in any way, you are giving that person or entity control over your mind, and it will have negative effects on your life.

Do you still think of the situations and dwell on what happened? Guess what? You are not hurting the person, entity or situation one bit. You are only hurting yourself.

You are causing that pain and getting yourself stuck. You have to decide to move forward, you have to decide to forgive. Even if the person or entity wanted to change what happened, they most likely can't. It means saying "Okay, this happened, but I have my entire life and future." There are enough pressures and issues in life in the present. Why do you want to carry around baggage from the past that you cannot change and which is holding you back from what you can be today and in the future?

Deal with it, heartfelt and mindfully, then move on with your life. Take the baggage and deal with it. You can take the wisdom, experience and enlightenment out of the baggage that make you better, then tie the baggage shut and dispose of it. And don't look back.

You deserve to let it go with no repeated thoughts, no dwelling, no bitterness or resentment. You have taken the good from the situation and the lesson has been learned. Now you can throw the rest away and focus on the present and future.

Before I go on, I plead with you not to take asking for forgiveness or forgiving lightly or do it halfway. Dive in 100 percent and it will make a big difference in your every day and overall life and long-term happiness.

Below is an example, but in many cases it would be better to take this template and add to it, so you can vent and let out everything you need to.

_____ *did*
_____*to me.*

This is how it made me feel.

This is what it did to me

*This is how I could have stopped, or minimized,
the above so it does not happen again.*

I chose to forgive them for the following reasons:

If you still have feelings that you have not
100 percent forgiven them, pray for them. It is
impossible, if you keep praying for them with a
pure heart, to hold onto that grudge.

Now think about these two tasks. While
they can be very difficult, imagine your life
without the guilt, bad feelings or bitterness. Think
about having no bad feelings toward anyone in the
world. It's an ongoing process, but not a daunting
task like the first time playing decades of catch up.
You have no guilt or blame. How awesome is that?

Last, but not least, there was someone who
did nothing to you and actually gave his life for
you, created you and gave you so many wonderful
gifts. That's Jesus, and it's time to ask for
forgiveness and repent.

Now that doesn't mean to keep doing it over, as repenting is asking for forgiveness and changing your actions and behaviors away from that. You will be amazed at what this will do for you.

Continue to self-reflect, to keep weight off you and forgiveness toward others. The peace in your life is worth the task. In the next chapters we continue to make a better life, a life wide open. And the good news above was the toughest part. Or at least it was for me. Congratulations.

Mindset

Let's first look at the issues, then the solutions.

Now many times that is where the advice stops. Change your mindset and poof ,your fixed.

While that is true, without correcting multiple connected things, you will not have long-term, sustainable happiness. The good news is it costs you nothing and you can start today.

In the following chapters you will see there are many connections throughout your mind, actions, body and nervous system.

Unconscious external events form beliefs, attitudes and behaviors, causing us to distort, delete and generalize what we take in in many ways. The term is VAKOG.

Visual
auditory
kinesthetic (feel)
olfactory (smell)
gastary (taste)

We take in huge amounts of data every second, while equipped to take in much less data. With our busy world, however, it is how it works. So, our brain adjusts.

As a result, we get greatly diminished versions of that data, which is why two people can have different versions of the same event. They each have different internal representations.

Internal dialog says it good, bad or to bury it. We filter it internally and our current state dictates it. So a bunch of ingredients go together for your internal dialog - logic, perception and illusion compared to facts.

If a dozen people see the same exact event and you separate them, there will be 12 different versions of the same event. Everyone's internal dialog processes events differently. That is why two people can watch a movie and one thinks it's great and one thinks it's terrible. Your version of any event is just that, your version, and it is important to keep that in mind.

Your unconscious does not process negative, and unless you change your mindset it stays negative and your perception is projection. No one can make you feel any way. You chose anger, sadness or happiness. Again, your perceptions are your projections.

Colossians 3:2 NIV
Set your mind on things above, not on earthly things.

The term "It takes one to know one" is so very true. But you can notice your behaviors, manage and control them, and get the results you desire.

You ever notice when you're happy, people around you seem happy, and when you're mad, all the people around you are in a bad mood? That is not always the truth. Many times you clone, mirror or reflect your internal state. Those people may be in a good mood but you are placing a reflection of yourself on them, so you can convince your belief system it's true. You must align and match your desires.

Now one thing to realize is it's not just your brain at work. It is a large collaboration, and your mind-body connection, and your nervous system all play a big role.

So, we know we delete and distort reality to our illusions in our unconscious mind. The great news is we also have control over what we do. Our attitude and personal power is our personal responsibility, crafting our life. Now how do we do that?

You choose that effect, or the lifestyle you live. It is not economic driven or geographically driven. It does not matter your age, or on anything that is going on around you. It is 100% self-driven. You have a choice, and once you accept that, you can live life wide open.

Romans 12:2 NIV
Do not conform to the pattern of this world, but be transformed by the renewing of your mind.

[this world...with all its evil and corruption. (See Gal. 1:4, 1Jn 2:15) Be transformed. Here a process, not a single event. The same Greek word is used in the transfiguration narratives. (Mt 17:2-

8; Mk 9:2-8) and in 2 Cor 3:18. Mind. Thought and will as they relate to morality (see 1:28; Eph 4:23). Then. After the spiritual transformation just described has taken place. God's will. What God wants from the believer here and now. Good. That which leads to the spiritual and moral growth of the Christian. Pleasing. To God, not necessarily to us. Perfect. No improvement can be made on the will of God.]

Are you negative? Does it seem you have a lot of negative things happen around you? Do you have negative people around you? Negativity will never make you happy. You will never have a happy career, life or family, with negative thoughts. They can never produce a good, effective life.

Negative people around you adjust and become just as negative. Whether it's you or other people, its toxic and will draw your energy and drain you. Negative people around you will drain you for their benefit.

The opposite is also true. If you are positive and surround yourself with positive people, you will create a positive life. This is true of all aspects positive - spiritual, happiness, successful, driven, persistent, outgoing. Whatever you desire is driven and controlled by you and your mind.

It is something you can start on today, but it takes focused, intentional thinking. You have been thinking the way you have for years, but in less than one month, through deliberately changing your mindset, you can create many more enjoyable thoughts, less stress and more powerful reality.

Mindset - Reset your mind

This is a huge topic and means many different things to many people and organizations. It is something you can start today and costs you nothing.

The mind can be a wonderful gift. It can excel you past your wildest dreams. It can be what puts you in bliss and makes every area of your life spectacular. It can also be a terrible thing where it kills dreams, careers, families, marriages, businesses and more.

Philippians 4:10-13
10 I rejoiced greatly in the Lord that at last you renewed your concern for me. Indeed, you were concerned, but you had no opportunity to show it. 11 I am not saying this because I am in need, for I have learned to be content whatever the circumstances. 12 I know what it is to be in need, and I know what it is to have plenty. I have learned the secret of being content in any and every situation, whether well-fed or hungry, whether living in plenty or in want. 13 I can do all this through him who gives me strength.

Where are you at? I can tell you this section can change your life, and it can start today. There are multiple sections coming that are really about mindsets also, but I will talk about this substantially because it has to do with everything you have read and will read. It has to do with every aspect of your life. I don't care how smart, spiritual, organized, temporarily wealthy or temporarily successful you are, it will never work long-term until you fix your mind. Likewise I do not care how disorganized, poor, unemployed, or how bad your situation is, with the proper mindset you can do whatever you want.

Isaiah 43:19
See, I am doing a new thing! Now it springs up; do you not perceive it? I am making a way in the wilderness and streams in the wasteland.

To have beautiful dreams you need a beautiful mind. Everyone's dreams and paths are different, but this is one truth that is a must. Think about the truth of how life can be, regardless of appearances. Fix your mind on that, believe it and take decisive action.

Many think that with a life going good your mind will adjust. This is not correct. You must first adjust your mind, then your life will begin to be good. When you change your thinking, you will start to see changes and evidence of your changes. You must change your mind in order for it to manifest.

Start thinking with clarity what you want. What are your goals that is your truth no matter your current lifestyle. You don't have to have it all figured out, just know what you want. At night you walk down the stairs in the dark and you can't see all the steps, but you trust they're still there. Driving at night your sight is limited, but you know the road goes beyond your headlights.

Now, some of the habits have to go. They're a waste of time. Let go of being a victim, the negativity, fear, drama, excuses, procrastination or whatever it is that's a waste of time.

Act as if it's yours already, and have a clear vision. We will begin in the next pages to work on the actions. But until you fix your mind, your path will be difficult. Once you correct your mind, your path will be cleared and your life will begin to move forward.

I tell you it will give your life so much power. It will uncomplicate your life, make your life easy and give you freedom. And is that not what everyone really wants?

Your thoughts dictate your life, good or bad. Focus on what you want, not what you don't have. With everything that comes into your life you have the choice of how to react and what you attract.

So start attracting good, not bad. Start being positive, not negative. Drop fear and procrastination and replace it with empowerment and action. Your life is waiting for your you. You have wasted yesterday ,but you can change your today.

Please don't think this will change overnight. It took you years to get this way, and you cannot snap your fingers and change it. It will take deliberately focusing on your thought process. But if you do it each day, it will get easier. You will have setbacks and bad days, but that gives you additional skills to adjust your mindset.

Take the chains off your mind and open it up to the possibilities. When you do this, you will see endless possibilities. Take away what you have just read about and start applying what you are about to read. Stop doubting and start knowing. It's all right there. You just have to change your mindset from I can't, to I can.

From negative to positive, whatever your mind is doing you are attracting. Your thoughts control you and your actions, so is it not best to attract what you want, how you want to feel, what you want to do? Go get it. It has all been waiting for you.

Change your mindset of limiting yourself because of money. There are many ways to move ahead without money. You can better your life, career, business and yourself with no money. So stop with the money mindset of being obsessed with money. Money is just one tool, and there are many tools that can move your life forward without money.

Self-affirmations work really well, and repeat them throughout the day to keep your mind in the right level. Some examples are.

It's all encompassed with many things in this book, so we will have two sections on this.

But know, as I am speaking from experience, this is something everyone can and should do.

Victim

Very rarely are we truly a victim, but many sure like to play the part. Once in a while in life there will be a case where you are the victim, but most of you are only a victim to your actions, or to what you allowed to happen. That is not being a victim, that is self-inflicted misery brought on by yourself. Trust me. You will see a true story below where I allowed self-inflicted misery.

There is such a victim mentality these days so that we do not have to live up to our full potential. So we don't have to take responsibilities for our actions. It's much easier to blame others than to look in the mirror and say "I did this to myself, I let this happen."

If you truly want the most out of life, stop playing the victim and start being the in control of your life. Think of the power that gives you. You can have anything you want, and you dictate that. If the people are around you bring you down, you are in control of that. Just because they exist does not mean you have to hang around them.

If you are broke, get another job, sell stuff, do what it takes to get you where you want to be. There are very few times in life where we are a victim, so stop feeling sorry for yourself, take control of all aspects and let God guide you to your path. No one else. It does not matter what you see as the hurdle, what matters is God has a predetermined path for you and it's not being a victim.

You can blame and focus on what others did to you or you can own what you did and learn and grow from it. In my last relationship my partner was an idiot. Well why did you date an idiot?

In the business deal they promised a 1000 percent return or I would not have done it. You knew a 1000 percent return was not likely, but your greed took over and you saw an easy way to make money. There is nothing worthwhile that's easy.

He or she is a psycho, is mean, is a liar or evil or whatever. You may be right, but there were signs you chose to ignore, advise you chose to ignore.

You put yourself and kept yourself in the situations. You allowed it, and now you want to be a victim, because it's a better story. You cannot change it, but you can choose to own it and not repeat it.

True life example

So, I am in my store one day and in walks a person. And after speaking with her I discover she just went through a traumatic event. I ended up asking her out, and after talking back and forth over several days she accepted. Things moved very quickly and we were pretty much inseparable.

While I was successful and happy I was, I thought, in need of a real and deep relationship. I know now, just as I kept seeking with my business to grow more and expand, it was because I was not on my true path.

At the time I thought I needed that in my life, and thought I had it. But it is not what I needed. I was very mistaken. But reflecting back on what happened to me over four years is pretty incredible, yet really sad and pathetic as to what I let happen to me and the way I allowed myself to be beaten down.

I moved in with her, and at the time she was drinking a lot. Things would be going well, then the drinking would start, and she would all of a sudden announce she was going to move across the country and pretty much say "I know it sucks for you, but it is what I need to do." She would sober up, then start drinking again. This was a recurring theme. Then later in the night she was going to move again.

One day later she came into my store. It

was a Saturday, and as you will see, Saturdays were not good many times for the relationship. She said she wanted to go to a children's birthday party with a friend, which sounded harmless enough.

Then she told me it was with a guy she had introduced me to at the time, who was dating a friend of hers, But she said since then their relationship was on rocky ground.

She assured me it was as friends, but that she was not bringing her children. Of course, I thought that was odd that she was not bringing her children to a child's birthday party. Looking back, I am not sure what the heck I was thinking during the next four years.

Anyway, she told me how much she loved me and left. I closed the store earlier than normal since it was Saturday. I went to the house, got her children and brought them to the park. I had sent her pictures, and the second flag went up as she screamed at me that I sent her pictures to make her feel guilty.

After the park we went home and there were pictures of her and the guy together posted on Facebook. Not at a party, but standing, posing as couples do. She had pretty much ignored my calls or texts all day. Then as it got later, I got a text asking if I minded going to my apartment because she wanted some alone time.

I messaged many times and tried calling, asking her to stop by but she didn't. The next day got more bizarre, and she was doing a lot of drinking. She said she got pulled over and I could not get a hold of her after that. I was worried and went to her house.

Thankfully, her car was in the driveway and I walked in. As I got to our bedroom, there was the guy with his suitcase, folding some of his clothes. She was in the next room and I asked her what was going on and if anything had happened.

She said no and he went out to the garage to smoke. I went out and asked him to be honest, and he confessed. I then went back inside and she denied it again until she found out he had told me. We talked, she flew into a rage, then calmed down. I had her make a choice.

She chose me, but asked if he could stay the night and do her tattoo. I said no and she asked me to drive him the 1½ hours home with her friend but she would not be coming. I can't believe I agreed, but I did. This started the slow downward spiral for the next four years.

There were real life events you would not find in your best fiction novels. I was warned by multiple family members, police, a therapist and friends. But out of ignorance and thinking I could fix it and make it better, I stayed. It is also more proof you can't make people see what they don't want to see.

I can say for certain, at the time, had I practiced self-evaluation and reflection, aligned my goals, path, mindset, self-imagined, focused and really looked at the encompassed purpose, the relationship would have been drastically different. But at the time I did not have the knowledge or tools. Now I do, and am sharing them with you.

Complaining/whining

Complaining many time comes from choices we made or comparing our lives to others. I don't want to go to work. I don't want to work 12 hours. I hate my job. These are choices you made and if you don't like your job, do what you need to do to get a new one. If you don't want to work 12 hours, get your life adjusted so you don't have to.

It might mean going back to school and working full-time. It might mean making less but fulfilled more. It might mean down-sizing or moving to where there are better opportunities. It might mean you have less, but life gives you more. It might mean taking that leap of faith to start living your dream.

Another example is Joe, who has everything. I can say, for a fact, that Joe was either born into or worked his butt off and struggles to get it. If you want to get it, then go get it. But it's not going to happen by complaining about it.

Can you imagine if Moses led the people to the water with an army behind him and said "crap, there is water blocking us, I am old and I don't have a boat. It's not really fair that others have a boat. Well I guess we are all going to die. Why does this always happen to me.?" No, he aligned himself with God, and the waters opened up and they crossed in a way not humanly possible.

Now tell me again why you can't work

hard and get more out of life. I don't feel sorry for you, and you have the knowledge to change any and all aspects of your life. Just ask for guidance and God will show you the way. Change and utilize the tools given throughout this book. Now stop complaining and start doing

Drama

This section will be very short. If you allow drama, if you create drama, if you participate in drama, stop. It's toxic and a waste of time and your life.

You have but one life. Why waste it participating in foolish behavior. There is nothing productive that comes out of drama, whether it is self-created or you are merely participating in it. You are the only reason you have drama around you, and you are the only one that can stop it.

Galations 5:15 NIV
If you bite and devour each other, watch out or you will be destroyed by each other. [bite and devour each other. The opposite of v 13-14. Seeking to attain status with God and human beings by mere observance of the law breeds a self-righteous, critical spirit.]

You create the drama. You have done drama and talked about others so your bad deeds and bad behavior is not recognized. With drama or without, the end results are the same. Except one way you look foolish and the other you let the end results speak for themselves.

Stop it now. It's a waste of your time and everything around you. It's an unnecessary way to make not only your life, but the ones around you, miserable. There is no need or excuse for drama, in most cases, unless you are acting in a play. If you are acting the drama part in life, you're wasting what could be a wonderful life.

Philippians 4:8 NIV
Finally, brothers and sisters, whatever is true, whatever is noble, whatever is right, whatever is pure, whatever is lovely, whatever is admirable - if anything is excellent or praiseworthy - think about such things.
[true...praiseworthy. Paul understood the influence of one's thoughts on one's life. What people allow to occupy their minds will sooner or later determine their speech and action. Paul's exhortation to "think about such things" is followed by a second exhortation, "put it into practice" (v9). The combination of virtues listed in v. 8-9 is sure to produce a wholesome thought pattern, which in turn will result in a life of moral and spiritual excellence.]

Excuses

Excuses sound best to the people making them up. You can have every excuse out there as to why you look the way you look, why your life is the way it is, why you got bad breaks, why you don't have time to do this or that, why you are not happy, why you don't have the job you want, the house you want, the car you want, why you have not moved up, why you are not as spiritual as you want to be.

Excuses are lies wrapped up in a nicer way. Most of the time it was not your priority, not important to you. So instead of you owning that you did not get the report done because you watched four hours of Game of Thrones, you make up an excuse how you tried to get it done but you had family things come up. You tried and all of a sudden there was a home invasion. They stole my report and I had to start over. In Game of Thrones maybe a dinosaur egg fell on your foot.

You are the reason. You can either keep giving excuses for yourself and your surroundings or you can pick yourself up and change it. And you can do it today. Don't give excuses, give action and effort, and always do your best. You can excel or have excuses, but you can't do both.

This goes back to self-reflection and mindsets. You have control over your life and you either do it or you don't. There is no need to appear weak and come up with an excuse. Own it, and whether you did or didn't, you will find the outcome is better with truth and accountability.

Fear

Fear is many people's nemeses, and it can paralyze you. It rarely is as bad as you imagine if it even exists at all. How many of you have *complained* about not getting a break, and when opportunities presenter themselves to you, you made *excuses* why not to do something out of *fear*.

Deuteronomy 31:6
Be strong and courageous. Do not be afraid or terrified because of them, for the Lord your God goes with you; he will never leave you nor forsake you.

[This was the Lord's exhortation, often through his servants, to the people of Israel to Joshua, to Solomon and to Hezekiah's military officers. By trusting in the Lord and obeying him, his followers would be victorious in spite of great obstacles. This applies to God's faithfulness in providing for the material needs of his people.]

You see, many aspects of your life ,positive or negative, are connected. Do it anyway. If you do it and fall flat on your face, you are still one step ahead of the person who never tried.

Embrace the fear and move past it. You can feel it, but don't let it stop you. Fear is a dream killer. Don't let the what ifs become the I should have done it or I should have tried. You have an opportunity to take on a fear. Do it and you will be a better person. And more than likely it will take you to the next level.

Do what's outside your focus and your comfort zone. Expand your life and live life wide open.

Worrying is fear's brother. How many times have you worried and lost sleep and the next day all you worried about was not as big as the torture you had put yourself through? Worrying fixes nothing and can be self-defeating. What's your worry? What can go wrong? What is worrying going to help?

Stop thinking that way. How about thinking "What good can come out of this? What will I learn? How can I make sure I don't worry about it again? And how can I make sure to make the best out of this situation."

Whether you worry or not, the situation is going to happen or not. Is it better to do the above – to be positive and learn from the situation rather than torturing yourself. Take charge, learn, grow and take corrective action.

You have control over your life, but not always the situations around you. Why worry about things beyond your control. If you are giving your all and doing your best, own it. You have tried, and worrying about it will not help one bit.

Reflect on why is this happening. What I mean by that is are you hanging around toxic people? Are you on the right path? Are you doing what needs to be done, or filling your day with fear and worry rather than action?

Procrastination

Do you get things done? Do you ever hesitate on opportunities? Do you ever procrastinate? Do you take action or dream of the life you can have and go back to social media or television for hours?

Do you take steps to improve yourself, or talk about taking steps to improve yourself? If you hesitate or procrastinate, you are stopping your growth. You are holding yourself back.

I can't really do that because . . . that's an *excuse.* I would get started on that but - *excuse.* I will wait and get fresh start tomorrow - *excuse.*

I could keep going with 100 examples, but you know. You also know we all do it or have done it. This is one of the biggest self-sabotaging act you can do. You can talk about your dreams forever, the life you want, and nothing is going to happen if you talk about it but don't act.

If you fail 100 times, you are way ahead of people that procrastinated and never tried. I can tell you that you will advance yourself from those experiences. I can tell you out of the 100 failures you will gain much and you will win in many ways.

What is stopping you? What is making you hesitate? Unqualified excuse. Do it anyway. You have to start somewhere, and if you are serious about having a better career, business or life, stop procrastinating, stop hesitating. Work with the facts and notice when you stop the process. Is it in the beginning, or when it starts getting difficult, or almost to the finish line? Once you start to realize your pattern, you can correct it. You can start to put tools in place to correct it.

Your self-image

Well congratulations if you made it this far. Now is what I feel is the awesome part. Dealing with the issues, improving and taking charge of your world. I have a very different view of self-image than many of the motivational things you have seen or read in the past.

2 Corinthians 5:11-12
11 Since we know what it is to fear the Lord, we try to persuade others. What we are is plain to God, and I hope it is also plain to your conscience. 12 We are not trying to commend ourselves to you again, but are giving you an opportunity to take pride in us, so that you can answer those who take pride in what is seen rather than in what is in the heart.
[take pride in what is seen...The pretension of the false apostles is a superficial front; their concern is not with spirituality that is true and deep, but with money, popularity and self-importance.]

You know what works for you so give it deep thought. If you're uncomfortable in a suit, why go out and buy an expensive suit. You don't have to, as some suggest, go out and buy a fancy car because you deserve it and it will make you successful.

Because of one of the businesses I own, I have access to very nice cars. You know what? I don't drive the nicest car, I drive the one I like the most. Truth be told, whenever I can I am on my motorcycle, not a car. Does that make me less successful? Of course not.

There is something to be said about making the choice to conform or not. No, you don't have to, but yes it makes it easier. I push the limits, and some people don't like my tattoos or hair, but it was a choice and I know I have to overcome the stereotype before some people can move on.

I do think it's wise to dress appropriate for the situation, because many people will not think "wow what a maverick," they will think "wow, he or she has no respect for what we are doing here."

That being said, it's your self-image. If material things are important to you, then by all means get them. What I am saying is hold your head up high and be the absolute best you can be. If that means you park your 1988 Pontiac in the back of the lot or around the block until you can upgrade, do it if it really bothers you. If it doesn't, park right next to the guy with a $700 a month car payment who is stressed every day because he should be driving an older car.

If that means you took the bus or walked, who cares? You showed up and are the Rolls Royce of you. If you are learning, growing and doing what needs to be done, everything will come, and there is no sense eating out of a can with a Mercedes in the driveway.

Don't compare yourself to others, you're you, and you have unique gifts no one else in the world has. You are the only you. Do not cause more stress in your life by overextending yourself. It will distract you and take away from true happiness and fulfillment and will stop you from reaching your goals as quickly as you could have.

We will cover this in upcoming pages. There are goals, procedures and plans to reach the next level. What is important is you being comfortable with your own skin and the level you are at. The level you are striving for should make you proud, confident and assured.

You are on your way to a better life, and no one can stop you but you. Really think about that the next time you are meeting with that executive and going after the big one. You are there, it just has not manifested itself yet.

Lastly, and most importantly, you have to love yourself. No matter where you are at, or what your situation is, love yourself for you. On the following pages if you're not there, we have some tools to help you.

Look in that mirror and smile knowing you are doing the best you can, the best you know how, and know it only gets better from here. Right now, stop and give yourself some love. Think about the unique things you offer the world and how amazing you are.

Being in the present

You need to plan, focus and dream in the future, but you don't live there. The past is the past. Let it go and learn from it. Nothing can be changed, and you have already made amends of any negative past experiences. So, let it go, you don't live there.

Don't look at the past as it's done and cannot be undone so don't dwell there. Learn from the message and move on. You have the present, yet most dwell in the past or focus fully in the future. No matter what your current issues are, what is happening right now, what are you doing right now, right this minute, it's not that bad. See it as better now. If you focus on the now, direct your attention on what you are doing and the facts instead of thoughts, you will be happier and much more productive.

Focus, and do the absolute best you can with what you are doing in the present. You will see many things happen, you will reduce your stress, and will increase the quality level of what you are doing.

You will find yourself getting more done and you, in turn, start to increase successes in your life. You can plan for the future, have goals and timelines and a list of to dos, but break down your plans to your top three. Then prioritize, select one and laser focus on that task at the present time. Don't think of all the things going on in the world.

That can wait. When you bring you self to the present, you can achieve more, do more and be happier doing it.

Stop what's stopping you

Stop the fear, doubt, self-loathing and pity parties. Stop making yourself a victim and start making yourself a victor. Stop with the excuses and procrastination. Just stop. Stop with the negative mindset and worry, bitterness and hatred. Stop it all - stop it now.

Proverbs 17:22
A cheerful heart is good medicine, but a crushed spirit dries up the bones.

Do not say a lack of money is stopping you. It's not. It is one thing out of a huge, abundant life, and you can get started without it. And if you do, you will realize and be able to prioritize money, because you don't need it.

You are why you are where you are. You are the reason. It's time to take responsibility for your actions and move forward. You, and you alone, have the power and it starts today. Knowledge is power you have and you can get the power now to get the life you deserve.

If there are roadblocks, stop and take a different road. If the people you put in your life are stopping you, then you need to make changes in those relationships. If your business, workload, finances or organizational structure is stopping you, change it.

You are able to stop what's stopping you from starting today. You can start a new direction and new path to start moving forward and progressing toward your goals.

If you truly take in the tools needed, you can start today and stop what's stopping you. You can start moving forward and start living the life of your dreams. You can start today.

Change

Well, this topic encompasses everything from the beginning to the end and more. The important thing to remember is you have to want it. Most resist it or fear it, and some plain do not like it. Secondly, you have to put in the work and do it. So many talk about changing, but few take the action needed to make it happen. It is not putting some post on Facebook, or telling people you are changing.

Philippians 1:9-11

9 And this is my prayer: that your love may abound more and more in knowledge and depth of insight. 10 so that you may be able to discern what is best and may be pure and blameless for the day of Christ 11 filled with the fruit of righteousness that comes through Jesus Christ – to the glory and praise of God.

[abound more and more. Real love requires growth and maturation. In knowledge . . . The way love grows. Depth of insight. Practical discernment and sensitivity. Christian love is not mere sentiment; it is rooted in knowledge and understanding.
Discern what is best . . . Christians are to approve what is morally and ethically superior. Pure and blameless . . . The goal of Christians in this life is

to be without any mixture of evil and to be open to censure because of moral or spiritual failure. Then the goal will be perfectly realized. Christians must give an account.

Filled with the fruit of righteousness . . . what is expected of all Christians. Produced by Christ through the work of the Holy Spirit. To the glory and praise of God. The ultimate goal of all that God does in believers]

I am sure you have heard that words actions speak louder than words. I know you have seen people that put on a good act at church or a social gathering and are not so nice outside of that environment. That is acting.

While I recommend affirmations to assist your mind to set changes, that is not the same as acting. You are training your mind for change and bettering yourself for the future. While you may have self-doubt at first, as the weeks go by you will see the inner change within you and it will begin to manifest an outward change.

The change I am speaking of starts in your mind and is manifest in every area of your life. You can be anything, do anything and it's not about telling anyone, it is about them noticing without you telling them.

It's about you doing the best you can do in all aspects of your life. The mediocre you is gone. You have been chosen for a purpose and a particular path on this earth, so live up to it, do it and change the things that need to be changed.

Show the world the unique gifts you have that no one else has.

Think of animals and insects, caterpillars turn to butterflies, mammals shed their old hair and adapt to the season, many animals grow and adapt to the size of their environment. How big are you going to let your environment be? You choose it and if your environment is not good, change it.

How do you spend your life? Your routines and behavior must be flexible. Most are change averse, and it is why many settle or become stuck. Your daily routines are just that, you're not free if you wake up, do your routine and go to bed. You have to want more. If it's not working, what changes do you have to make to get to the life of your dreams?

You need flexibility to change it. If you are in the dark in a strange environment and you hit a wall, you can either stand there and wait for the wall to open, ignore it and wander around, or you can change your path until you find the door. Once you find the door, open up your possibilities. You are familiar with your surroundings now and can now walk through and focus on the new doorways.

So think of your goals. Is that what you really want? If not, reframe it. How are you going to achieve the change?

Now pain is a fast motivator, but it fades. For example, you go to pet a dog and it bites your hand. You are very motivated to move your hand quickly. It's not pleasant, and once the pain goes, you stop moving your hand.

You ever notice when there is an emergency how you come up with money (car repair, rent, etc.)? This is really a reaction and not change.

Change is using all the tools in this book and anywhere you can learn, and being happy and motivated, no matter how long the journey takes. You have clarity in the end result of how you will change and what you are out to receive, and a clear path on the steps you will take or create to get there.

Do everything you want to do. Don't let fear stop you, go for it, and if you fall or stumble, who cares? It's happened before and you will get up and push forward. Don't be like the majority, who die with so much of their life yet to live. But they never lived. Live your life, your dreams, your calling and nothing can stop you but you.

You have everything you need to start on that change, but that journey is up to you. So get off that couch or chair and start living life to the fullest. Be the best you can be and live life wide open.

Take time out for yourself – alone time

This is very important. In the morning and at night I set aside time for myself. In the morning I wake up with gratitude and thank Jesus for all he has done in my life. I think of many things during that time, from being thankful I opened my eyes, to the blessings that surround every one of us.

You need this time of gratitude and focus. Some people jump up, get in the shower, throw on clothes, rush to work and sit down. Their head is still spinning and they are no way prepared for the task, the day, or anything. They have just wasted the last hour in a panic, chaotic, unorganized rush mode and have no clue as to what the day holds more than they did when they woke up.

Now think of this. You get up and shower, pick your favorite spot to sit that morning and give thanks and gratitude for everything that has been and will be. You focus on how wonderful the blessings you have are. Take some time for deep meditation. Then you have yourself in a place where you can properly focus. Focus, and plan your day, then take your happy self to meet the day.

I have had people say I can't I get up at 6:30, then the children get up, dog, excuse, excuse, excuse. Get up at 5:30 then. It may be tough for a few days, but once you begin this process you will see it's so valuable.

During the day, when you feel it starting to build, take a moment to breathe. Just stop, breathe, give gratitude and if it's too much, ask for God's help. He is always there for you. Then refocus, adjust and take on the day.

When you end your day, think of all you have your loved ones, how wonderful your life is and the direction you are headed. Think of the people in your life who have been blessings, the wisdom God is giving you and the blessings you will have tomorrow.

Think of all the good things you can do and how you have been given the gifts to do them. Once you are in that state you will see how great you sleep and rest. It is a proper way to pray, and you will find you are truly blessed.

Boundaries

You have to do this. There are many people out there who are draining you of what you could be. There are people who will use all your time for their benefit if you let them. There are the energy drainers who have such a negative, screwed up view, and they will beat you down if you let them.

There are things you are doing that are doing to yourself - time wasters and busy work - when you could be doing things more productive. Stop, reflect and readjust. Stay in the present and focus.

You have to set boundaries. You have to adjust who are with and what you are doing. You owe no explanation. You have to do what you need to do to get yourself on track.

I have gone through this before I had the knowledge I have now, and I could go into some stories that would make you say WOW. I let myself go from a focused, optimistic person to over years being beat down to a lump on the couch before I finally woke up and said something is wrong, enough is enough.

With my life at that time, I should have either stopped after the first time she cheated, or at least established boundaries. The second or third time, and so on. At that point it is really not a matter of love, but of how much the person is willing to trash your life.

If they are screaming, downgrading or plain

cruel every day, you have to set boundaries. This is not healthy, and it is not good for you. So set boundaries now.

You must come to the realization not everyone is on your side and not everyone is looking for your best interest. That may include you sometimes. You have to wake up, and certain people and things have to stop.

They will try to suck you back into their miser, but don't let them. I am not talking about a friend in need. Of course you should help them. Instead, I am talking of needy, self-righteous, self-victims who don't value what you are doing. I am talking about your activities that are not worthwhile. Get rid of it and don't let people and things dictate how you live and what you do with your life. It's your life, they are your goals and dreams. Get the toxic things and people out of your life right now. If you are self-sabotaging, set up boundaries for yourself.

Lastly, there are good intentioned people who want you to do things for them. There is nothing wrong with this, but it is when it gets to be a daily routine - "do this for me because I don't want to," or "I don't feel comfortable doing this." For one, they are saying their time is more important than yours, and they are saying it's okay if you feel uncomfortable. Lastly, they are saying I don't want to grow, I don't want to change, and I don't want to achieve on my own. If you truly care about this person, please handle this not in a way they might not like the most, but in a way that will help them the most.

The biggest thing with helping everyone day in and day out is that your dreams, goals and achievements start to get squeezed out for theirs. I am not talking occasionally helping someone in need. Of course, we should help. I am talking about everyday tasks that people ask you to take on, so they don't have to.

Make sure to guard your time, priorities and boundaries to serve God and yourself at the highest level.

What if?

Start with the what ifs. What if I just did it? What if I failed? What if I succeed? What if I live my dreams? What if I do my path? What if I go for it? What if I go to the next level? What if I start living a purpose-filled life? What if I live with a great attitude? What if I was focused? What if I stop the drama and excuses? What if I cut out the toxic? What if I had priorities? What if I made my self-accountable? What if I lived my life with gratitude? What if I did my best? What if I learn and grow? What if I get help on my journey? What if I had more discipline? What if I stopped wasting my time? What if I have balance? What if I am courageous? What if I acknowledge God for his great gifts daily? What if I allow myself to be guided? What if I surround myself with good people? What if I live life as a beginner? What if I take away my self-limiting beliefs? What if I live life wide open?

Isn't it wonderful to think about? You may have noticed the above is not all sunshine and rainbows. What it does is show is when you take out the crap, excuses and setbacks. You can be happy and life is good and easier if you do the above. We are only on this earth for a short time, so make the most of it while you are here.

Align your destiny

Dream and be guided on your path and plan. Set goals then smash them. Do the grind it takes to make them happen. It takes work though, as no one is going to hand you your dreams. Make sure your dreams and calling are aligned.

You can have plans and goals, but they must align with God's vision for you. He had a plan and destiny for you before you were you. He is a God of free will, so you can choose to do what you want. However, that path will only have temporary successes and many obstacles.

2 Corinthians 5:13-19

13 If we are "out of our mind," as some people say, it is for God; if we are in our right mind, it is for you. 14 For Christ's love compels us, because we are convinced that one died for all, and therefore all died.15 And he died for all, that those who live should no longer live for themselves but for him who died for them and was raised again.16 So from now on we regard no one from a worldly point of view. Though we once regarded Christ in this way, we do so no longer. 17 Therefore, if anyone is in Christ, the new creation has come. The old one has gone, the new is here! 18 All this is from God, who reconciled us to himself through Christ and gave us the ministry of reconciliation:19 that God was reconciling the world to himself in Christ, not counting people's sins against them. And he has committed to us the message of reconciliation.

He will let you choose, but you will keep being guided to the path he has chosen. Have you ever had the feeling there has to be more than this? Have you ever been called to do something different but for whatever reason you did not?

If this is recurring, you have to ask yourself if you are aligned. Do you get happy and feel fulfilled when you think of doing it?

Maybe you are a CEO of a large corporation and every day you are filled with chaos and dread, or maybe just not feeling fulfilled, and you have had recurring thoughts of how nice it would be to open a deli. You think people would think you're crazy, so you have never pursued it. It might mean a lifestyle adjustment or taking a chance, but if that is your destiny, your path and what you are guided to, it will make you fulfilled and happy. What is stopping you?

Live your dreams, live your calling. You will never have happiness and fulfillment until you do. Maybe you are a mechanic and you have a calling to be a doctor, maybe a lawyer and have a calling to be a pastor, a sales executive but really want to be a stay-at-home parent, a stay-at-home parent but really want to be landscaper or a pilot. Whatever it is, do it. Nothing is stopping you but you.

Now there is a truth you can accept or not

accept. Your path was created before you were born. Have you ever seen money-hungry people who never have enough, people who switch jobs a lot, marriages or relationships, or places they live, even moving from state to state, thinking that will do it?

No matter what they do, they're never content and always searching, always wanting more. I can think of one time someone told me God told them what to do but they didn't do it. Gee, I wonder why they have issues.

Corinthians 5:20-21

20 We are therefore Christ's ambassadors, as though God were making his appeal through us. We implore you on Christ's behalf: be reconciled to God. 21 God made him who had no sin to be sin for us, so that in him we might become the righteousness of God.

[Christ's ambassadors. The honor of Christ and his church is in his ambassador's hands. He expects them to represent him well. People will think more highly or less highly of Christ and his church based on the effectiveness of his ambassadors' service. A summary of the gospel. Christ, the only entirely righteous one, took our sin upon himself at Calvary and endured the punishment we deserved, namely death and separation from God. Thus, by a marvelous exchange, he made it possible for us to receive his

righteousness and thereby be reconciled to God.

I will bring up another case. There was a guest pastor who came to speak at a church. She called this boy out and said very nice things. She said God spoke to her and told her this boy would be a minster.

Let's just say the boy was misguided and followed in a haphazard way, then went the opposite direction. He had great successes, but always temporary, was always searching and never satisfied. For him was something empty within.

He was in a relationship where he had been beaten down so bad that it finally dawned on him he had to fix it ,or at least fix himself. He started reading self-help books and it helped.

All of a sudden, he started feeling an urge toward God. He started growing and getting closer to God. Then out of the blue got a calling from God that put his life in a totally different direction. It was not a whisper, but a very powerful and serious nudge. What it is was not totally clear, and as he went he thought of the stories I shared a few pages back about the stairs, or headlights, and clarity happened as he followed in faith.

Now that guy was me at 50, yep 50. You can say what you want, and believe what you want, but I chose to go against it for years, never understanding why I always had stumbling blocks or roadblocks, or why I would come to cliffs that plain stopped everything. I will tell you I do not know.

Think about how powerful that is. God has a plan and a purpose for your life. It has always been there, and that is why you do not need to see all the steps. When you get aligned with God, he will guide you.

It won't be all sunshine and rainbows, but when it is rough, if you are aligned, you can give it to God. You will be content.

Go do it

You can sit all day and make excuses as to why not, or you can do it. If you are a homeless and want to be a home builder, pick yourself up and work toward that goal.

Maybe your dream requires schooling and you have to work and go to night school or online classes. No matter what it takes, if you want it, there is a way to get it.

Start now and take the steps to do what you want to do in life. No matter the task, climb the mountain one step at a time and there is nothing stopping you.

There is no reason you can't start today. You may start with baby steps, but that is okay. Maybe it's not a life-shattering accomplishment, but a movement toward a better life. A start, and the persistence to keep going every day is a huge accomplishment.

You may have wasted yesterday, but that does not mean you cannot start living a purpose-filled life today. It's your time and your journey, so do it, make it happen, go for it. Be the best and make it happen.

Plan – Overview of life/work

This is very important and something many of us, including me, struggle with. It will, however, organize your life and make it easier. It also frees your mind from the clutter of what has to be done. It makes it clear what is important and what is not, what your priorities are and what can wait.

Without plans you have an entire life of to dos, some of which are not worth your time, but because you don't have a plan, you are always a step behind in chaos - not planning ahead and focused, with a clear vision is ahead.

If you have no plans, your present is a mess. You must relieve yourself of the chaos strategize and plan, then let it go. You will know what to do. You have laid out the steps you know, and have a clear vision of how to get there. Things may change along the way, but you can change and adjust with them.

I tell you again, from experience, your plan must be aligned. If your plan is not aligned with the plan God has already designed for you, I do not care what your resources are - your intelligence or ambition - if you go against God you will at the most only have temporarily achieve success that will crumble.

James 4:13-17 NIV Now listen, you who say,

"Today and tomorrow we will go this or that city, spend a year there, carry on business and make money." 14. Why, you do not even know what will happen tomorrow. What is your life? You are a mist that appears for a little while and then vanishes. 15. Instead you ought to say, "If it is the Lords will, we will live and do this or that." 16. As it is, you boast and brag. All such boasting is evil. 4:13-16 It is good to have goals, but goals will disappoint us if we leave God out of them. There is no point in making plans as though God does not exist, because the future is in his hands. What would you like to be doing 10 years from now? One year from now? Tomorrow? How will you react if God steps in and rearranges your plans? Plan ahead, but hold your plans loosely. Put God's desires at the center of your planning; he will never disappoint you.

First, I would recommend reading through this book in full. Your plans and lists are not just writing down a list of stuff to do.

Start with your goals, both personal and business-related, and set aside time to focus on this. Be honest with yourself and be realistic about where you are starting, but think big. Then do an action plan on how you will reach these goals. You need to write a plan you can believe in and stick to.

Before you start, what kind of person do you want to become, what is your purpose, what will give you peace and full fulfillment? State what it will look like, and be specific, right down to your image at that time, lif style, focus, family, spiritual, balance, career, recreational time, financial and self-wealth (which does not mean money). What is your present situation and what steps will you take to get to your goals?

Now break it down. It should be all-encompassing because if your life is not balanced, it won't lead to the life you can sustain or be happy and fulfilled with.

I will give you some key points that have worked very well, but it depends somewhat on your task for the day. If you are taking on a large task, of course there is less on your list. But certain days there will be many small things that you can get through in no time.

For example, simplify it, but keep in mind the top three are your main priority. Then three to six and six to nine, and so on.

Do not make a large list because doing this instantly becomes overwhelming. There is always much to do, and by picking out your top three it makes it manageable and also makes it quick and easy to review. You will also find the things on the bottom of your list changing or taking care of themselves.

So, you have your goals and plans for life. Now take all the things you want to accomplish this week and list them out. Be realistic. Do not have 100 things on your list.

Now you are ready for your daily list.

Start mornings with a quiet time of gratitude.
Work/Secondary
1.
2.
3.
Family/ recreational
1.
2.
3.
Goal actions
1.
2.
3.
Quiet time to reflect and give thanks.

Long-term goals
1. By _____ I want to send my children to private school. I will make $10,000 more a year to make that happen.
2. I want to in _____ buy a boat, go on a missions trip or take my family on a nice vacation. To do that, I will start saving_____ a month to fulfill my goal.

Then make it happen. Do what it takes. Later, we

will work on one year, 60-day and 30-day goals.
I have also included many tools in the back of the
book for this.

Focus

Focus on your priorities and what will give you the life you want. That might mean not spending hours on Facebook. That might mean not numbing your mind by watching hours of TV on the couch. That might mean working smarter and harder and focusing on what you have to do to accomplish your goals.

Proverbs 4:25 NIV Let your eyes look straight ahead, fix your gaze directly before you.
Proverbs 4:23-27 Our heart-our feelings of love and desire dictates to a great extent how we live because we always find time to do what we enjoy. Solomon tells us to guard our hearts above all else, making sure to constrain on those desires that will keep us on the right path, Make sure your affections push you in the right direction. Put boundaries on your desires and don't go after everything you see. Look straight ahead, keep your eyes fixed on your goal and don't get sidetracked on detours that lead to sin.

It might mean more time at church and less at the bar. It may mean a lot of things. Focus on you, your goals and your plans to achieve those goals. When you're at home, be home-focused on family and recreation. When you're at work, focus on working.

In the world today it's very easy to lose focus and get distracted, but electronic devices, phones, social media, the internet, television, associates, friends, family, day dreams, random thoughts and your career. But it is important to stay focused and do what you are doing, not the other 100 things around you.

If you stay focused, many things will happen. You will get more done and your spouse and children will actually get to spend quality time with you.

Your career will also excel as you improve your quality and time management. It does not matter what the task you have chosen, focus on that and give it your best. You will find that all of a sudden the task that used to drag on can be done quickly. You will see your family grow closer, and you will find that you have additional time. Your life deserves your focus and attention, as do the things around you.

No excuses

This is a big thing, and usually ties into victim mentalities. He or she did this to me, so this happened. No, you let him or her do this to you, so this happened. I almost had it finished then_____ happened, so I was unable to finish on time. No, you didn't finish on time because you did not set enough time aside to make sure the task could be finished.

This section could be pages and pages, because people love their excuses. It's not okay.

It is this simple. If you truly want to get ahead in any aspect of your life, stop make excuses and start owning it. You and you alone can be stalled out and have great excuses why, or you can move ahead. Stop the excuses, conquer life and move your life to the next level.

You can make excuses or you can change. You can be accountable and take responsibility for your actions. You control your priorities you control your time, and you control how fast you get to your desired end results.

So why don't people and organizations do it? The truth is it's easier to make excuses or blame others for ourselves. It is not always fun to own everything, but it is needed. You need to own your life and all parts of it. You can achieve incredible things, but excuses have to go and honesty and accountability must start.

Accountability

This is something you absolutely need, and most do not have. They have negative traits, so they avoid accountability. This is a tough thing to own.

It's much easier to blame or make lame excuses than to own your accountability. But once you do, it is incredible. It is incredible for many reasons. But to start, you are doing something a large majority of the world does not do.

You have joined the group of an elite few who are taking control of their lives. Owning all aspects, good and bad. This is rare, and trust me people will notice when you take accountability. It puts you in the forefront, builds trust and loyalty. It makes you stand out from the crowd, as people are playing the blame game or making excuses and you are leading the pack. It is not always easy, but it is always worth it.

Time Lie

Whether you are homeless or a billionaire, we all have the same 24 hours, the same 1,440 minutes, the same 86,400 seconds in a day. So many say I just don't have the time. No, you would rather do something else than that task.

You wish you could be more involved, but with this and that, I just don't have the time. This leads back to two things - excuses and accountability. It does not sound as good as saying I am sorry about the orphans Edith, but I would rather go home and watch hours of television.

Time is available for your priorities and if not, change it so it is. You do not have to do anything you don't want to if is not a priority to you, but own it and do your priorities. Stop wasting your time and saying you have none.

Every second and minute counts, as you only have so many. You make the choices you do on how to spend every moment of your life. Are your seconds and minutes being spent in a worthwhile manner?

Are they fulfilling your life's dreams and goals? Are they moving you closer to where you want to be? Do not fill your day with busy work and dead time that can be spent doing what is going to take your life to the next level.

Wealth

When I speak of wealth, I am not only speaking of money. There are many ways to be wealthy in this world. There are many ways to be happy and penniless. Too many confuse happiness with money, and it's not. It's a tool, like everything else. That tool can make you or break you. There's so much more to life than money, and money is not wealth.

Many have asked "why do the motivation books? Focus on money. That is simple to answer - it sells books. The first part of this book has some tough self-truths. This is not always popular or easy to take in, but they are truths that will make you live an encompassed, purposeful life.

2 Corinthians 9:6-7 NIV
6 Remember this: Whoever sows sparingly will also reap sparingly, and whoever sows generously will also reap generously. 7 Each of you should give what you have decided in your heart to give, not reluctantly or under compulsion.

Money is not evil or good. The people who have it are evil or good. Your attitude toward it is good or bad. You have to develop a good mindset or you will not attract any type of wealth. If you want money, it's there, but you have to ask yourself if that's what you really want.

Let me explain. If you want money and you think money is no good, or you think as a poor person does, you will not have any, or not for long. If your wealth is you want a loving wife or husband but you think negatively all the time and are not sure if you are good enough or they are good enough, you will never have a loving spouse, or not for long.

You see, again it gets back to your viewpoint and mindset. Be what you want to attract and do what you want to be. You can't sit on the couch eating a bag of chips and think if I was not so out of shape I would exercise and lose weight. Guess what? You are never going to exercise and lose weight.

1 Timothy 6:10 NIV
For the love of money is a root of all kinds of evil. Some people, eager for money, have wandered from the faith and pierced themselves with many griefs.

Money cannot be your God. Some desire money more than God and try to hold on to it more than God. If they do that, how low of a priority is their family, friends or anyone? They put a piece a paper before God and wonder why there not fulfilled. Imagine if they sought God and tried to hang on that tight? And if the world did that it would be a wonderful world.

1 Timothy 6:17-19 NIV
*17 Command those who are rich in this present
world not to be arrogant nor to put their hope in
wealth, which is so uncertain, but to put their hope
in God, who richly provides us with everything for
our enjoyment. 18 Command them to do good, to
be rich in good deeds, and to be generous and
willing to share. 19 In this way they will lay up
treasure for themselves as a firm foundation for
the coming age, so that they may take hold of the
life that is truly life.*

You can't expect a wonderful family,
business, career, money, happiness, spirituality,
joy and all the other things that bring you wealth
and fulfillment while wanting one thing and
thinking and doing another.

Align your mind and actions. Then you will
have an abundant life. I will tell you that money is
not all that, and is a very small part of a happy,
fulfilled life. It is a tool, and maybe you need it for
your purpose and maybe you don't.

It is attainable through alignment and
action if that is what you need. But it is a very
small part of a plan when you analyze it. There are
many unrelated steps to be done, but some people
just concentrate on getting money and miss all the
other steps.

Many times, it is used as an excuse. I
would if I had the money. I can't afford that. I
wish I had the kind of money to do that. Now for

truth. I am going to get a second job, new clients and work toward that promotion to acquire the monetary tool that allows me to get that. It is my goal and I will do X, Y and Z to accomplish it. It will take_____ to reach my goal of getting____. If it's worth it, you will do it, if not, you won't.

So no matter what your wealth is, you can have it and there is nothing wrong with it. What you have to be careful with, is your mindset. Don't make it your idol, guide or god. There are plenty of rich and poor people in the Bible, and plenty of good rich and poor people today.

There is wealth beyond money. You should have all of it, no matter what it is, and enjoy your encompassed purpose with all the tools given.

People and Peers

You are making these fabulous changes, and everyone will be so excited for you, right? WRONG. Hang on, because if you truly step up and make changes for the better, some of your loved ones, friends and colleagues that you thought would be your biggest fans will not be.

When you start on your journey they may say you can't do that, or what's this about. Insecurities creep in for them and some will do anything in their power to stop you.

Some will leave your life. Some will get distant. While this is difficult, it is also good. It allows you to know you are changing. It allows you to upgrade who you surround yourself with.

I would much rather be alone than be around some of the people that distanced themselves or left my life when I began my journey. And I am very selective who is in my circle because for me, moral character and the way you treat others is much more important to me than if you have a million dollars.

Do the best you can do, be the best you can be, and you will lose people along the way. But you will gain others and grow, and it is so spectacular that your only regret will be you did not know sooner.

Priorities

You have to know, implement and develop your priorities. What is that you want? What is it that will get you there? And what steps will you take to get you there? That might mean changing up stuff and stopping boys'/girls' night out, or at least getting home at a decent time. It means less wasted time and more focused time, It might mean a lifestyle change. It might mean you start getting up earlier to make it happen.

Now as your journey develops, and as you grow, your priorities will most likely shift, change and evolve. What I thought my priorities were when I started my journey are not even in the top 10 anymore. Some are gone altogether. So as with many things, your plans are fluid and should be reviewed often. That does not mean giving up on something because it's hard. It means as you grow and change, so will your priorities. Throughout this book you have been asked to do things, and all the lists and plans should be checked on and advanced as you advance.

No matter what, you must have a list of your priorities, because it affects so many other aspects of your life. There is no right or wrong, and they can be moved up or down, or new ones added and others taken away.

Below is a list, one through 10, with one

being the most important. I would recommend reading through the entire book. Look through anything and review. Then start the process from the beginning of the book.

Priorities
What is it?

What is your plan to get it?

What is the timeframe?

Do your best, but do something

There is never a perfect time. There is never a perfect circumstance. How many times have you had a great thought or idea and talked yourself out of it? I hate this job. I should leave and do_____. Then you talk yourself out of it.

The world today is so negative and filled with doubt and fear. Do it. If there is an opportunity and you know it can lead to your desires, dreams and maybe even the path to your destiny, go after it.

Proverbs 19:21
Many are the plans in a person's heart, but it is the Lord's purpose that prevails.

It does not mean you have to change your life around. But begin to take steps to do what you want to do, and be who you want to be. Stop dreaming about it. Start living it. Start doing it.

At first maybe you have to take baby steps, and that is fine. The important part is to start. Nothing can happen until you try. Give your dreams and goals effort and action and begin to explore the life you want, instead of the life you are living.

Take steps today toward the life you have been thinking about and hoping for. It is time to start taking action. Make a movement toward it. Now is the time, today is the day.

People ask why I am not blessed with this or that. God created you, and gave you a path. Now imagine you're God and for 40 years he has been throwing you hints and nudges, and you're a 40-year-old gamer that binge watches whatever and your idea of exercise is to go to the kitchen and back to the couch.

God will bless you for eternity, but you have to take action. God gave you unique gifts and a brain to use them. God gave you everything you need, yet if it feels like something is missing? It is time for self-reflection. I bet you will find you have hindered, self-sabotaged and untrained yourself. God is waiting and has been there for you, waiting until you finally decided to get started. Not next week, not tomorrow, TODAY!!!

Live life as a beginner

You ever noticed someone who has all the answers? Is it you? You try to explain different things, but in their mind they are sure they know, and will tell you even when they are clueless. This is something that tends to happen backwards from age. Somewhere in your teenage years you have mastered life and figured everything out.

1 Corinthians 4:1-3 NIV
1 This, then, is how you ought to regard us: as servants of Christ and as those entrusted with the mysteries God has revealed. 2 Now it is required that those who have been given a trust must prove faithful. 3 I care very little if I am judged by you or by any human court; indeed, I do not even judge myself. 4 My conscience is clear, but that does not make me innocent. It is the Lord who judges me. Things that human wisdom could not discover but that are now revealed by God to his people.]

This lasts into your 20s, as you begin to find out you don't have it all figured out. Or it might even be in your 30s, when all of a sudden you start to recall advice and information given to you.

In your 40s or 50s, you realize you don't know everything and discover how much you have yet to learn. And if you're lucky, you start to live life like a beginner.

The good news is you don't have to wait. You can jump ahead of the curve and here is how. Set your ego, pride and self-righteousness down and slowly walk away. It's that simple.

If you don't believe me, ask people in these age groups, and at any age talk to people older than you, people in their 70s, 80s or 90s. They have vast knowledge and experience, and will share it if you ask.

What do you do when you're a beginner? You look for wisdom and guidance, and educate yourself on how to do it. Somewhere after learning to tie our own shoes and age 20, we tend to lose the ability to be humble and remember we have to learn and grow daily.

This is such an amazing thing when you can have the self-realization that you don't have all of the answers and have a lot of questions to get to the level of wisdom you desire.

Live life in every aspect as a beginner. Be open to learning and hearing new things, different perspectives and different ways of getting things done. Once you open yourself to new possibilities, to taking advantage of wisdom being offered to you, you will see why living life as a beginner is so mind opening. It is a true path to real wisdom.

Learn from others – learn, learn, learn

This is very important, and again a way for you to set yourself apart. I suggest daily reading, learning videos or go to school. Whatever your desire is, learn and educate yourself daily.

John 13:15-17
15 I have set you an example, that you should do as I have done for you. 16 Very truly I tell you, no servant is greater than his master, nor is a messenger greater than the one who sent him. 17 Now that you know these things, you will be blessed if you do them.

You have the opportunity to make yourself better every day. There is no reason not to learn as libraries, online courses and local colleges all have the tools to help.

If you cannot afford school, start at the library and better yourself until you can. There are also apprenticeship available. If you know what you want to do, start to work in a company. You can do that. Maybe it's not the position you wanted, but you can learn the position and skills, and transition to the desired position.

Positive mental manifestation

Now some people frown hearing this. This does not mean you will always be skipping down the street singing about rainbows. This means you are deciding not to be miserable.

Think of when you're mad or sad and have a big sour face. You're hunched over, your shoulders are slumped down, and you feel dark, empty and miserable. You are not going to feel good about yourself, and eventually the people around you.

Now think about when you are smiling. Your posture is good, your shoulders are back, and you feel like you are ready to take on the day. You're laughing and joking with those around you. Your day is fun, not like dragging a rock around under a big storm cloud.

Now let's face it. It is not easy. According to the National Science Foundation, 80 percent of your thoughts will be negative at first, 95 percent are repetitive, and we have 12,000 to 60,000 thoughts a day. A great way to begin retraining your brain is affirmations.

Studies show that in as little as 21 days your brain starts to retrain itself. I am not going to lie. Depending on where you are at right now, it will be hard, and takes conscious thought, controlled and deliberate thoughts, and eliminating and transitioning the thoughts you do not want. It took decades to get this way, and you can change it in 21 days or soon after. Isn't that amazing news?

Philippians 3:16
Only let us live up to what we have already attained.

[Put into practice the truth they have already comprehended. We are responsible for the truth we already possess.] Change your mind and it will change your life.

Misbelief, behaviors and procrastination can be turned into an encompassed path and a new journey. Just how fast is up to you, but it's amazing to know you can evolve and change your life in less than a month, if you really want to.

Gratitude

If I had to say, one of the most important aspects to growth, goals and dreams would be gratitude. I do not care what your current situation is. There is so much to be thankful for, so much to appreciate.

Luke 6:38
Give, and it will be given to you. A good measure, pressed down, shaken together and running over, will be poured into your lap. For with the measure you use, it will be measured to you.

There are miracles and unbelievable things all around you, all the time, if you would just pull your head up from your negative state, stop and look around. From the minute God opens your eyes every morning, there are gifts and miracles all day long that you have nothing to do with.

Everyday, God gives you gifts, starting with the gift of life. From waking you up in the morning and giving you another day to shelter, birds, nature, health, food, family, friends, and even the stranger who walks buy and gives you a sincere smile.

There are also big things like children and grandchildren, your partner, your path, your church and his scripture that provides all the answers. Even if someone is nasty to you, be grateful that you live right and are not like them.

This list of things to be grateful for every day could be hundreds of pages long. Look at the world around you and really pay attention about everything. Then you will notice what you have taken for granted.

Open your eyes daily and be thankful for the blessings and miracles and give him and others gratitude. And what you have to be thankful for will multiply.

Give

This is such a wonderful gift to give to yourself, and if you don't, you will never have a fulfilled life. Now this is where many reading go "I can't make ends meet now and you want me to give? For starters, to give can mean many things - your time, effort or friendship to a person in need.

Now there are two ways to give, the right way and the wrong way. First the wrong. If you are giving in any way to be seen giving, you are not truly giving. You are networking and marketing yourself, and branding your image to fit what you want people to think of you.

Matthew 6:1-4

Be careful not to practice your righteousness in front of others, to be seen by them. If you do, you will have no reward from your Father in heaven. 2 So when you give to the needy, do not announce it with trumpets, as the hypocrites do in the synagogues and on the streets, to be honored by others. Truly I tell you, they have received their reward in full. 3 But when you give to the needy, do not let your left hand know what your right hand is doing, 4 so that your giving may be in secret. Then your Father, who sees what is done in secret, will reward you.

[This verse introduces the discussion of three acts

*of righteousness: giving, praying and fasting.
Jesus' concern here is with the motives behind
such acts. Spiritual growth and maturity - or
perhaps a heavenly reward of some kind – or both.
One should not call attention to one's giving. Self-
glorification is always a present danger.]*

If you are giving with the thought that I
will give to him or her, but they better remember
this when I need x, y or z, that is not giving. That
is bartering or buying favors. Or you could even
think of it as buying goods and services.

The right way to give means you do it from
the heart, even when no one is watching you do it
and you get nothing in return. You give from your
heart and soul. You give in a non-judging manner.
You give all the time, and you give for you, not for
any other reason. Just because you want to give.

Now back to the monetary part of giving,
because it's the hardest for most people to do. You
make $500 a week and you decide to start tithing
at church. Again not because you feel obligated or
guilty, or you want people to see you, but because
you are giving from the heart.

Proverbs 11:24-25
*24 One person gives freely, yet gains even more;
another withholds unduly, but comes to poverty. 25
A generous person will prosper; whoever refreshes
others will be refreshed.*

[Generosity is the path to blessing and further prosperity. By contrast, the stingy do not make friends and hurt themselves in the long run.]

The problem is your head says I want to give, and I can afford it this week, but man that is $50 out of my $500 paycheck. It would be different if I made a million dollars a year. Would it? Would it be easy for you to give away $100,000. No, it would not because it's the same percentage.

I am not saying if your lights are getting shut off not to pay the bill and go give all your money away and it will come back to you. What I am saying is give as much as can, the best you can, in whatever way you can. It will come back to you many times over.

It will improve your feelings, your mental state and your pocket book. We all need to give and be generous. In doing so you can make the world a better place for you and others.

Kick butt!

Don't get your toes wet, go all in, 100 percent. Give it your best, then get better and give it more. It does not matter what it is, give it your all.

Amaze people, not with talk, but with action. If you tell me about how much you are doing and how you are doing great things, I can almost guarantee you are doing busy work and not kicking butt.

If you were, you don't have to tell anyone anything. They see it and tell you. Don't quit when you're tired, take a break and get back up and stop when you're done.

Acts 20:35
In everything I did, I showed you that by this kind of hard work, we must help the weak, remembering the words the Lord Jesus himself said: 'It is more blessed to give than to receive.'

It's amazing when you get aligned, encompassed and working together how much you can accomplish, and how much you can do in a short amount of time. So grab life and shake it, live every moment, take it all in and give it all you got.

Action

You can have the best tools, but they will not fix your car, You can have a nice car, but it won't drive itself, You can have a key to your house, but it won't unlock itself. It takes you being in control and taking action to make it happen.

Make the changes you want to make, live better and change your beliefs. Internal change has to happen before anything else. Then you are unstoppable, you have personal power, you have more and do more.

1 Thessalonians 4:11-12
11 And to make it your ambition to lead a quiet life: You should mind your own business and work with your hands, just as we told you, 12 so that your daily life may win the respect of outsiders and so that you will not be dependent on anybody.

Know your outcome, target your objective and know what you really want. Now I will almost guarantee this will change, because what you see at first as your goal is really a step to what you really want. So analyze what you really want. I want a million dollars. Why do you want that? So I have enough money for my dreams. What are your dreams? I want a big house on the water. Your goal is not a million dollars, it's the house on the water.

Now that you know that, you know your target. Now envision it and experience it as if it has happened. How does it feel, touch or smell? What feeling does it give you inside? If you truly feel it's your goal, it is easier. You know the outcome and you know what you want. You don't need to know all the steps it will take, but you can now begin to make a step toward it. You can look and say "is this helping me get to my end goal?"

How have people who have had the same goal achieved it? Now do that. It takes massive action and if what you are doing does not achieve your goal, stop and take it out of the equation. Not busy work, real focused attention.

So, ask yourself does it really need to get done? Does it really matter for the goal for your life? What's taking up your time? Don't let fear inside of you control your drive and state of mind. You should have your goals and dreams listed, and everything else is secondary. You are now starting to envision your encompassed purpose and beginning to think of steps to work on it.

I recently heard this and think it's genius. Get out a pad and paper, we are going to make a list. Now without over-thinking, first write down the number one thing on your list.

Okay, now that is it. Time moves quickly, and when your time is gone, it's gone forever. Accomplish your number one goal, then move on. Don't plan forever and don't wait forever. There is no reason not to start taking action today.

Embrace your new you

No matter who you are or your situation, embrace the new you. Embrace the dream until it becomes a reality. If your new dream requires schooling, do it. If requires learning, do it. If it requires you breaking out of your comfort zone, do it. If it means changing friends who support your dream, do it.

You will never get ahead thinking about it and dreaming, It takes action and hard work. It takes doing whatever it takes to achieve what you want to be.

You need to align everything to the new you and stay focused. You need to decide you want to be better so you will be better, and become the new you. No matter what the circumstances, use all the tools to remain on your path.

Move ahead with what you see as the end result. Feel it, taste it, visualize it, and most importantly pray about it, to make sure your path is aligned with what God has chosen for you.

You again have a choice, but only one long-term solution. What is the new you? What have you been created for? What are your unique gifts and talents? Stop and ask yourself the above, then get started living the new you.

Listen to the inner voice

Have you made plans, carried them out and failed? Have you had every obstacle thrown in front of you? Have you had a plan where it just has to work and didn't?

Psalms 33.11 NIV But the plans of the Lord stand firm forever. The purposes of his heart through all generations.

> *"The plans of the Lord stand firm forever" Are you frustrated by inconsistencies you see in others, or even yourself? God is completely trustworthy - his intentions never change. There is a promise that good and perfect gifts come to us from the Creator, who never change.*
> *(James1:17) When you wonder if there is anyone in whom you can trust, remember God is completely consistent. Let him counsel you, trust in his plans for your life.*

God gives us the choice of free will. He will allow you to whatever, but that does not mean he is not going to guide you to the path he created for you before you were born.

You can make millions of dollars and be

successful, but you will always crave more. You will never have a fulfilled, aligned, or wide open life without him.

That doesn't mean his path will allows be easy. It just means it will be right. It means he will give you purpose to live out your destiny. He will guide you, sometimes near and sometimes fa, but he will always be there for you.

He has always been there for you, but for some people, including me, it takes longer to wake up and realize our plans don't matter.

Hebrews 6:19
We have this hope as an anchor for the soul, firm and secure. It enters the inner sanctuary behind the curtain.

[Like an anchor, holding a ship safely in position, our hope in Christ guarantees our safety. Whereas the ship's anchor goes down to the ocean bed, the Christian's anchor goes up into the true, heavenly sanctuary.]

There was, and is, a plan for us already set, and you can either go with what you were designed for, or keep picking your own direction. I will tell you, however, since I have chosen to follow his path I have never been more happy, fulfilled and content. I, with his guidance, have developed an encompassed purpose, and it's been spectacular.

You can go from worry to being stress free, from wondering to knowing, from emptiness and chasing chaos to fulfillment and peace. You can go from fear to fearless and knowing whatever happens is in his hands and he has chosen you, recognizing your unique talents to do what he has called you to do.

John 1:3-5

3 Through him all things were made; without him nothing was made that has been made. 4 In him was life, and that life was the light of all mankind. 5 The light shines in the darkness, and the darkness has not overcome it.

[Life...one of the great concepts of this Gospel. The Greek word for "life" is found 36 times in John, while no other NT book uses it more than 17 times. Life is Christ's gift and he, in fact, is "the Life." Light of all mankind...The gospel also links light with Christ, from whom comes all spiritual illumination. He is the "light of the world," who holds out wonderful hope for humanity and for the creation. Darkness...the stark contrast between light and darkness is a striking theme in this Gospel.]

God created you for a unique purpose, to do something in this world that was designed for you to give to the world. God picked you. Do you see how powerful that is? We should all wake up and spend every moment of the day and night giving him gratitude and thanks.

Beliefs

Beliefs are not real without faith and trust. They guide our values. Beliefs can be dead wrong and proven dead wrong, and people will still hold onto them. Beliefs take no knowledge and require no logic. A belief can stand, no matter if it's true or not.

Beliefs are can be true or self-fulfilling prophecies, and guide behaviors of the subconscious. Beliefs say I can do it, or I can't, and both are correct, dependant upon your belief.

If you change belief, you change behavior. The noncontinuous brain receives a lot of data every second. It constructs sees, hears, feels, deletes, distorts and filters. Your beliefs and intentions matter.

Let your unconscious brain take information. There are several functions of the brain, and it does vastly different things. Harness your power, learn and expand your vision. Your attitude, personal responsibility, communication, report, connections and the crafting of your life are all the cause and effect equation.

Cause is personal power and accountability. Effect is being a victim and blaming. This cause and effect develops all of our decisions. Most people are on the effect side. You have to shift your mind to the cause side of being responsible for your actions.

Do you say I am a victim or that it is his or her fault? That's effect thinking. Or do you say I am the reason for my outcomes and only I can create my future? That's cause behavior.

You see cause gives you control over your life and effect gives others control. You are in charge of successful achievement of your goals. It's time to take charge of your life and be an adult.

Couscous and unconscious decisions have led you to where you are now. If you feel bad about what someone has done to you, it is you doing that to yourself. You have power you're your emotions and you are not a victim. If you're sad, you control that, if you're happy, you control that. You can say "That person make me angry, sad, mad, happy, annoyed or whatever." But I am here to tell you they don't. You feel that way because you choose to feel that way and you need to take responsibility and own that.

You have a choice how you respond. You can either let them control you or you can have control over you. So, take your beliefs and empower them.

I can think of many times in my life when I have had a belief that was off. Maybe I assumed and believed a person with wealth was greedy, only to find out they were more generous than me.

Maybe you had a belief about a political party. A type or brand of car or motorcycle, or a type of person. These are stereotyped beliefs. Maybe you believed you are better than another because you sin differently.

Have you believed something very strongly, and through experience, education or life-based knowledge found out that belief was wrong.

We need beliefs, however if you are not open to accepting truths and open to gaining knowledge to see if your belief is misguided, you're a fool.

The key is to take beliefs and either dispel them as wrong, or gain full knowledge of them so you don't believe but know.

I used to believe in God, yet rejected him and did not seek the truth. Much of what I thought was misguided, misaligned and just plain wrong. I now live as a beginner, seek knowledge daily and no longer believe what I thought or what people have told me.

I have gained, or am gaining knowledge, not of others' opinions or indoctrination, not from a sect of Christianity, not from twisted opinions to meet others' beliefs or agendas, but what God wants and what God has said. I don't have to believe, because I know. It's directly from him, and he has had it all written down for us. No matter how Man tries to twist it, the truth is the truth.

Now think of some silly beliefs you feel strongly about. This car maker is the best. This motorcycle is the best. These shoes are the best. Or this state or community is the best.

No. They just have very good marketing

that appeals to you, and you have talked your way into it, created thoughts and been indoctrinated. But if you think about it, how silly is it that you get mad when someone is not liking your preference? They have either not been indoctrinated or have been indoctrinated by another company or brand.

Hold your beliefs but limit them, and have the goal of moving that belief to either letting go or to full-blown knowledge.

Higher Power

You can choose to believe this or not, and many books refer to it as a higher power of the universe, or whatever. I have had a calling multiple times in my life but have gone the other direction, denied it, ignored it or resisted it.

Finally, through multiple events and for multiple reasons I pulled my head out of the sand. God gave me a wakeup call I could not deny. He gave me a clear and concise path I was to follow. It was so loud and powerful it was really a "wow" moment and was not to be ignored.

I have run a business full-time, learned and studied about God and gone back to school. I have had an amazing journey and life-transforming experience.

2 Timothy 3:16 NIV
All scripture is God-breathed and is useful for teaching, rebuking, correcting and training in righteousness, so that the servant of God may be thoroughly equipped for every good work.
[All scripture. The primary reference is to the OT, since some of the NT books had not even been written at this time. God-breathed. Paul affirms God's active involvement in the writing of scripture, an involvement so powerful and pervasive that what is written is the infallible and authoritative word of God.]

To go back a bit in the book, there was the negative situation where I allowed myself to go from positive and focused to slowly, over four years, being beaten down by someone until I finally had a wakeup call. This wakeup call turned my life back to amazing, and made my life so wonderful, not only for a while, but for eternity.

Through my journey I want to help as many people as possible with my time left here on earth. There is a higher power and he created the universe. He is God and his son is Jesus Christ and we were given the Holy Spirit. God saved us because we cannot seem to get it together as a human race.

Your road with God will not be all daisies and rainbows, but the changes he will make in your life are amazing. Let him guide and direct you.

Many people mistakenly think God is a genie and our wish is his command. That is backwards thinking. God will provide, but we are here to serve him, not for him to serve us.

You are unique in this world, and there is only one you. Think about that. Out of millions, God made you, created you and had your life mapped out for a specific mission and path before you were in your mother's womb. He could have made anyone, but he chose to make you. Realize what a gift that is.

You may be saying "well I don't feel

chosen." Well that is because God is a God of free will, and he will allow you to make choices, good or bad. He will allow you to do dumb things. Trust me, I have been there. I will tell you something. God wants you to pray, to talk to him, to give yourself to him. He wants you to let the Holy Spirit in and work through you.

Romans 8:26-27
26 In the same way, the Spirit helps us in our weakness. We do not know what we ought to pray for, but the Spirit himself intercedes for us through wordless groans. 27 And he who searches our hearts knows the mind of the Spirit, because the Spirit intercedes for God's people in accordance with the will of God.

[in the same way...As hope sustains believers when they suffer, so the Holy Spirit helps them when they pray. Through wordless groans...in v 23 it is the believer who groans, where it is the Holy Spirit. Whether Paul means words that are unspoken or words that cannot be expressed in human language is not clear- probably the former, though v27 seems to suggest the latter. The relationship between the Holy Spirit and God the Father is so close that the Holy Spirit's prayers need not be audible. God knows his every thought.]

Once you truly start the walk and have the

trinity in your life, you will feel foolish for the years you have wasted. The truth is the truth. You can know it, or deny it, but it is the truth and the way.

On average, we are only here less than 100 years out of eternity. This is our preschool or kindergarten for things to come. For sports fan, this is our little league to practice and get better at what we do, to follow our path around the bases to get to our purpose, which is home plate. What is your home plate? What do you feel called to do? This is where you give it your very best, follow God, know God and walk in the way you are intended.

Courage

Life takes courage, but not as much as we blow it up to be. We manipulate courage into fear or peer pressure. Here's what I mean. What if I do it and fail? That is fear. Courage, on the other hand, is "if I do it and fail, I am still a step ahead of the guy or gal that never tried."

Psalm 18:2
The Lord is my rock, my fortress and my deliverer, my God is my rock, in whom I take refuge, my shield and the horn of my salvation, my stronghold.
[Rock. The translation of two different Hebrew words "rock" is a common poetic figure for God, symbolizing his unfailing strength as a fortress refuge or as deliverer.]

Courage is having enough strength that when you see no light, and everything is the darkest, you have enough inside you to keep going and push through for the rewards.

Peer pressure is talked about a lot with younger people, but we adults have it too. If I stop being a CEO, senator, or whatever it is, and tell people I want to sell flowers on the corner, they won't talk to me anymore.

You could be right. But guess what? If you want to sell flowers on a corner, if that is your dream and they don't support your happiness, do you really want them around?

Are they really true friends, or is your status and money what they are friends with?

Joshua 1:9

Have I not commanded you? Be strong and courageous. Do not be afraid, do not be discouraged, for the Lord your God will be with you wherever you go.

Courage is saying "I feel I would love to sell flowers on the corner, and I am going to be the best flower person there is. I am going to learn a new occupation, market it and give families beautiful flowers."

Discipline – Performance – Goals

So many people want what they want but don't discipline themselves enough to get it. They dream and talk about it, but don't do the things they have to do. You have to have discipline if you want to grow your company or your life. No one will work as hard at it as you.

Jeremiah 29:11
"For I know the plans I have for you", declare the Lord, "plans to prosper you and not to harm you, plans to give you hope and a future."

There is a lot that could be said about a person not wanting to work hard at it. I would only suggest a new direction that you will like and will work hard at.

It does not matter what it is (business, home, family, spirituality, physical fitness, etc.), it all takes discipline and hard work. Not busy work, but performance-driven work with the efficiency and self-discipline to improve and become more efficient.

You need the drive to take you to the next level and the persistence to keep going when you're tired. You need the passion to carry you through tough times and to the end goals you envisioned from the start.

The more you align yourself and increase your discipline, performance, efficiency and knowledge and put in the hard work to get to the level that makes you aligned, with everything working in harmony, at first can be a bit much.

You know what though? You can do it. And if you focus and have discipline, you will do it. And you will be able to see your accomplishments and the mountain you climbed to get you to the next level. There will be the fulfillment and happiness of knowing you worked through the grind, corrected your actions, bettered yourself and championed whatever it was you wanted to do.

Always do your best and don't settle for less, or you will receive less. If want it, go get it, and invest in your skill set, mindset, and straight out discipline. Outperform and have persistence like no other until you reach your goals.

Focus and be in the present, with self-reflection for alignment. Be on the right track and take the right steps to make it happen. You know your path, and you alone are the one to get you there. Your encompassed purpose, if it has not already to come to light will, and your want, need and calling will be unstoppable.

Gut instinct

There is much to be said about your gut instinct. As you develop and align yourself, you will develop a gut instinct. The fact is you get that feeling, but can override it with greed, lust or bad judgment.

Galatians 5:18-23
18 But if you are led by the Spirit, you are not under the law. 19 The acts of the flesh are obvious: sexual immorality, impurity and debauchery, 20 idolatry and witchcraft; hatred, discord, jealousy, fits of rage, selfish ambition, dissensions, factions 21 and envy; drunkenness, orgies, and the like. I warn you, as I did before, that those who live like this will not inherit the kingdom of God. 22 But the fruit of the Spirit is love, joy, peace, forbearance, kindness, goodness, faithfulness, 23 gentleness and self-control. Against such things these is no law.

[not under the law…Not under the bondage of trying to please God by minute observance of the law for salvation or sanctification.
Christian character is produced by the Holy Spirit, not by the mere moral discipline of trying to live by the law. Paul makes it clear that justification by faith does not result in libertinism. The indwelling

135

of the Holy Spirit produces Christian virtues in the believer's life.]

You see, you are smarter than you want to admit. And as you know, or as you develop and pay attention to your instinct, you will see you have an instant knowledge built in. You can go against it, but much like going against God, it doesn't go well.

Leadership and servitude

Leadership and servitude are very similar. That is not a typo. They should be very similar. Why? There are many leaders, CEOs or heads of organizations who are comfortable making decisions. But they are not comfortable with accountability, responsibility or the consequences of their decisions.

John 17:17 NIV
Sanctify them by the truth; your word is the truth. [Sanctify, the truth, your word. Sanctification and revelation (as recorded in the word of God) go together. For the relationship between Christ's teaching and truth.]

There is one particular executive who comes to mind that is unlike anything I have ever witnessed. He is surrounded by "yes" people when he makes a mistake or needs to take responsibility for a decision that does not go his way. He has an automatic response to point fingers and try to either blame others, or at minimum to get someone to share the responsibility of his decision.

With this person we know ahead of time almost the exact conversation before the conversation starts. It is someone multiple people in one of my companies have had to deal with.

Independently, many people have come to the same conclusion and have a 1-4 system with him. What is the 1-4 system? You explain the situation, and no matter what it is or if he made a decision on his own in the middle of the Antarctic, within the first four sentences he will either blame someone, or in some way say he not solely responsible. He has never made it past four sentences, and it's been years and other organizations much longer.

Romans 12:8
If it is to encourage, then give encouragement; if it is giving, then give generously; if it is to lead, do it diligently; if it is to show mercy, do it cheerfully.

Do you want to be known as that kind of leader? That, for one is not being a leader. A leader takes responsibility, and a leader will take on a servant role or a leadership role. It's not about the position, it's about the organization, mission, path, family, church, etc.

Leadership is not a title or name, it's a behavior. It's discipline, and affects people around you, whether it's good or bad.

A true leader is gifted with collaboration, not fear. A true leader has discipline, responsibility and lives and walks as a leader. If your idea is leadership at all cost, no matter what, to get what you want, you're not a leader, you're a dictator.

If you live lavishly while others suffer, you're not a leader. You are not even close. If people, family members, employees or peers work with you because they have to, rather than they want to, you are not a leader.

If money is more important than people, then I have a surprise for you. People are nice to you because they pity you, not because you are a leader. The only ones who do not are the same pathetic people of similar minds who worship money as you do.

If people surround you for only monetary reasons, you are not a leader, and you do not have many loyal people around you.

Leaders bring out the best in others. They lift others up. They help others succeed. And their main drive is helping others, not themselves. They get to be leaders by giving, not taking.

Leaders are servants when they should be, and have leadership skills at proper times. Leadership has very little to do with your occupation, and a large amount to do with your life.

A great leader will be pointed out and acknowledged, and a bought leader has titles and initials before or after their name. A great leader will be for the cause and do what it takes. A bought leader gives orders from their office. A true leader is encompassed and driven by things greater than themselves. You see, a leader has to walk their truth. And if they do, it shows.

Destiny, dreams and pathway

In the past section on the higher power I touched upon this. You can have millions of dollars, mansions and be the CEO of a fortune company, but still always want more. You always feel unfulfilled, like you are missing something and there has to be something more.

Ephesians 3:16-20
16 I pray that out of his glorious riches he may strengthen you with power through his Spirit in your inner being, 17 so that Christ may swell in your hearts through faith. And I pray that you, being rooted and established in love, 18 may have power, together with all the Lord's holy people, to grasp how wide and long and high and deep is the love of Christ, 19 and to know this love that surpasses knowledge - that you may be filled to the measure of all the fullness of God. 20 Now to him who is able to do immeasurably more than all we can ask or imagine, according to his power that is at work within us.

[dwell…be completely at home. Christ was already present in Ephesian believers' lives.
Hearts…the whole inner being. Surpasses knowledge…Not unknowable, but so great that it

cannot be completely known. Fullness…God, who is infinite in all his attributes, allows us to draw on his resources –in this case, his love. Immeasurably more. Has specific reference to the matters presented in this section of Ephesians but is not limited to these.]

It is a pretty good sign you are not on God's path if you have not fulfilled your purpose to reach your destiny. It's up to you how long you fight and ignore the feelings. Some people do it their whole life, grasping for more, grasping for what they are missing.

You have your dream awaiting you, and if you just allow the thing you've had in your mind for decades, that keeps popping up on occasion, to happen, you will see a divine change.

You may be thinking pastor or missionary? Not necessarily. God has a plan for you, but it may be a writer, clerk, politician, teacher, commercial fisherman, parent or circus clown. It could be a multitude of things. That is for you and God to discuss. I just know it's there, and for true happiness, fulfillment, peace and so much more, you need to seek it out.

You should take a list of your top three. Now without overthinking, prioritize them. Whatever number one is, if you focus on that, one of two things will happen. 1. Your lower priorities will fall into place. Your lower goals will evolve, with some dropping off and new ones coming in as you develop your life. 2. What you thought you wanted is not what you really wanted and you have additional clarity and are one step closer to your dream.

Coach, Mentor, Consultants

This is a tricky subject, because in full disclosure I am all three. I also have all three. I will tell you having these will help your life tremendously.

First, I will start with some sad truths. Sadly, people who need this the most generally won't do it, come up with every excuse why not. Then in five years they will have plenty of excuses and blame why they are stuck in the same place they were five years ago. But they will be there until they stop resisting and wake up.

For those of you ready for a change to take your life to the next level, to improve on your life, this chapter is for you.
But first a word of caution. There are more books and programs on how to make money in these industries than there are at how to be good at it.

If the person you see wants you to be a victim, dwell in the past or blame everyone else, these are some red flags. They are looking after their pocketbook and not your recovery, change or growth anytime soon. They know they can keep you in this behavior for a long time, which equals many sessions and money.

Interview them first or get a free initial consultation. And if they do not want to do that, you saved yourself a lot of time.

Coaches are there to help you reach your goals, hold you accountable and change thoughts and behaviors that hold you back. Now with that being said, you have to be ready for real change or nothing will make it happen.

Coaches, mentors and consultants are generally not doctors, trained to deal with psychological items that need to be dealt with. They should always refer you for a diagnosis and treatment out of the scope of their profession.

A Coach - A coach is different than a standard counselor. A good coach is going to help you focus out of what's stopping you, help you focus on dealing and getting rid of the negative mindset and change it to a positive, productive mindset. They help you take what you are seeking to the next level and help you determine your true goals and aspirations. In short, they get you out of the rut, unstuck and on a focused path to achieve the life or business you hope for.

A Mentor – First, respect the time this person is giving to help you. They are doing you a favor and a kind act, so share your gratitude and make sure it is time used to gain knowledge and the best use of the time for both of you.

Depending on what you are seeking, you may need multiple mentors, or secondary mentors. A great business person may be terrible at family issues, and many times are.

They may be a great mentor at family

matters, but if you are looking to get more productive at work, that person has little value of work as their main focus is their family.

So plan ahead. There are great people, with many focuses, who are willing to share their knowledge,

Consultants – Consultants are totally different than the above. Consultants wants facts and numbers and do what it takes to improve those numbers. Consultants are there to fix what needs fixing, to make recommendations and even help implement those recommendations.

Consultants are generally fact-based, and because of what you hired them to do, can seem disconnected from people. You hired them for a task. They have to perform what you hired them for, and if that means elimination, consolidation, organization, growth, staging or whatever it is, that is what they do and what you want them to do.

At times you may need all three of the above. At times two, and maybe at times one. If you don't utilize at least one or two of these at all times, you are doing yourself a huge disservice. You don't have all the answers. I don't have all the answers. Only God has all the answers, and if you have tools to improve your life, do it.

If it makes you get to your goals more quickly, why would you not to do it? The biggest excuse I hear is I can't afford it. If it costs you a fraction of the return on investment (ROI), which is proven, that is just an excuse. The truth is, fear or dreaded change is what you may not be ready for. If you truly want to move ahead, invest in yourself. Your ROI on this is huge, and the benefits are huge, if you really want better do it and start very soon.

Don't do it alone

You're not a superhero so get help - employees, contractors, housekeepers, or whatever. The first thing I usually hear is . . .

1. I wish I could afford it. This by the same people who could be focusing on their business or career and possible achieving thousands of dollars. But instead they are losing four hours purchasing supplies, changing the oil in their own vehicle, then cleaning up and taking the oil to be disposed of because they save $12, compared to having someone do it.
2. I hired a housekeeper for two weeks and got a lot more done. It was only $60 a week and improved my work and home life. But I didn't like the way she did not dust behind my dresser.
3. Truth be told, you could dust behind your dresser in a minute   or two or you could mention it to the cleaner. You either have control issues or are self-sabotaging. Either way, you need to fix that.

Stick to what you are good at, and enjoy, and leave the rest to someone else. And don't say you can't afford it. You can't afford it because you are doing the task instead of what's important.

If you own the company and miss calls from customers because you are vacuuming the office, changing oil or filing, can you afford not to hire an employee or get help?

Balance your life

Please read the above again if you are trying to be a superhero and missing your children grow up or neglecting your spouse. You are not leading a sustainable life. Something will break down - your marriage, kids, work or all the above.

Your life, work and recreation must all be balanced.

Encompassed Goals

Envision - you smell it, see it and taste it. You see, if done, you feel it put your subconscious to work for you. Have you ever tried to think of a movie title, then hours later it comes to you? Your subconscious was working on it. Your mindset can do that with your goals. Create it, envision it and know everything about your goal.

Proverbs 4:26
Give careful thought to the paths for your feet and be steadfast in all your ways.

Need - What's your need, desire, end results, outcomes, specifics, need for others? Now, not later, with no hesitation, no doubts, no negatives, no to-dos, no self-sabotage from the past, present or future. Is the goal worthwhile? Does it meet your needs and desired outcomes?

Calculations - Who, what, when? Track your

progress, outcomes, time limits and time management. Get it all down so it's set in black and white. You need commitment at the deepest level for follow through, for when it gets tough and for when it is accomplished. Get whatever you need ahead of time so it gets accomplished.

Overcome - Be unstoppable and plan for roadblocks, and how you will overcome them. A roadblock is not the end, just an alternative path. So, plan in advance to overcome obstacles. Be flexible, learn from the lesson, gain knowledge and receive the blessings from it.

Massive action - Your initial action and change, even if it's a small step, is massive. Make it massive – dive off the cliff, burn the bridge, jump off that diving board, go head-first. Indecision kills goals, so go all in.

Plan, purpose, prioritize, positive, passion, pleasure, present text - no procrastination.

Achieve, accomplish., accountable. Is the goal

in reach? If not, how can you make it feasible? Is it too easy? You want it to challenge your capabilities. You also want it to be achievable, and if it's not, start on goals that make your goal achievable. How so?

Specific, defined goals, action. Who, what, where, why. Desires, do's, drive. Is it aligned?

Sustainable, agreed to, long-term, measurable, reward systems, small changes, small steps, substantial change, realistic, preset milestones that allow long-term success. Lifestyle not a race.

Before you start on the actual goals, know that if you won't make changes it's a waste of time.

Proverbs 17:24
A discerning person keeps wisdom in view, but a fool's eyes' wander to the ends of the earth.
[Fools "chase fantasies" and are interested in everything except wisdom]

You must set clear goals. You need to know it,

have clarity and avoid wasting time. You must brainstorm, research, stop obstacles and limit beliefs that are stopping you. If you truly want your goal, or goals, there can be no negative thoughts about it Know it instead of hoping or dreaming about it. Picture your end goal and really think about what it looks like, what your desired outcomes are. It takes change, action and work.

Get help. Think what you can accomplish, then imagine help and imagine what four or six people may accomplish. What's the purpose of goal? Are you ready to calibrate behavior to achieve your goal? Are you willing to shift your perspective, align your vocabulary, actions and behaviors? It all starts internally, and will manifest externally.

Proverbs 4:27
Do not turn to the right or the left; keep your foot from evil.

Let's start bridging from a want to a feasible goal that is reality. What can I do today to start on my goal, small changes that help you align and achieve your goal? Who do I need to be and what's holding me back? Until you really want it, until you're ready to dig in, it's not a true goal. It is something you leisurely want. If it's a true goal, analyze everything about it and act today.

Encompassed Purpose

It means it's time to live your life, not exist like you have no control over your actions. You're accountable, and you have an obligation to fulfill. You have limited time on this earth and it's go time, no more talk.

Psalm 119:105
Your word is a lamp for my feet, a light on my path.
[lamp…light. Apart from which I could only grope about in the darkness.]

It's time to master your past, align your path, dreams, passion and destiny. It starts internally. Before anything else can change, you have to change internally. And once that has begun, which can start right now, so can everything else.

You will not change like a light switch. You have had mindsets, thoughts, beliefs and behaviors your entire life. You can, however, get started today. You will begin to know the peace and fulfillment you should have had your entire life.

You may have wasted your life to this point. It does not mean it has to continue.

2 Corinthians 5:5-10
5 Now the one who has fashioned us for this very

purpose is God, who has given us the Spirit as a deposit, guaranteeing what is to come. 6 Therefore we are always confident and know that as long as we are at home in the body we are away from the Lord.7 For we live by faith, not by sight. 8 We are confident, I say, and would prefer to be away from the body and at home with the Lord. 9 So we make it our goal to please him, whether we are at home in the body or away from it. 10 For we must all appear before the judgment seat of Christ, so that each of us may receive what is due us for the things done while in the body, whether good or bad.

[God...has given us the spirit. The Holy Spirit applies the benefits of Christ's redeeming work to the hearts of believers and makes his resurrection power a reality of their daily experience. This guarantees their eventual transformation into the likeness of Christ's glorified body]

There are some simple procedures to do, and I tried to make them so they work for the internal changes, business changes, spiritual changes, family changes. No matter what it is, they all start with this process. You will know instead of hope. You will know instead of dream.

1. **Idea:** What is it you want to do? What is the change, the growth, the advancement you want to make? If it's, say, to buy a new house or expand your business, or grow

155

spiritually in the next year. First, make sure it's clear and that you have clarity on what you exactly want.

2. **Brainstorm:** Okay, take five minutes and just as fast as you can write down every question, every idea to make it happen, benefits, purpose, what you will stop, what you will start, positives and actionable steps. There should be no negatives. If you do not have clarity and purpose, do not worry about that. We can work on that in a bit.

3. **Research:** Reflect on your idea and brain storming results? Do you have a different perspective now? Is it clear? Is your idea what you thought it was, or after reflecting is it the same? If not, repeat with your new idea until you have clarity on your idea and what you want the end result to be. For this, I will give you a startup business example. This is just an overview of some of the questions.

    1. How will you market the company, products or services?
    2. How will you monetize? What are the price points and profit margins? And if you do not know, research the industry, competitors and suppliers, and you will be able to fill in the blanks.
    3. Who are successful people in the

industry and what are they doing? If you stumble upon struggling companies, what are they doing or not doing.

4. Looking at your company, what are similar companies offering, and what company or companies would you want to model?

5. Can you explain your product, service or company in under 30 seconds?

6. What capital would be needed and how will you achieve that?

7. After dissecting all this, is further research needed? If so, break it down until it's clear and you can picture yourself with the end result desired.

Act

1. When and where?
2. Accountability. If you hired a coach, great. If not, pick out three people who are easy-going, don't criticize and question what you are doing and understand if you get off track. These people should like all of your ideas and, for the most part, what you do. Okay, do you have your three names?

   Great. Now crumple it up and throw it in the garbage and pick out real accountability partners who will hold you accountable, will question you and keep you on track and accountable to your time lines, etc.

1. Are any obstacles stopping you, and if so, how do you overcome them?
2. What is your desired outcome?
3. What do you need?
4. What's your ultimate desire?
5. What are your weekly goals?
6. What are your 30-day goals?
7. What are your 60-day goals?
8. What are your long-term, one-year goals?
9. Know your accountability check-ins and schedule for that.
10. Arrange for daily accountability and alarms for

reminders.

Let's start with your weekly, 30-day, 60-day and yearly goals. The weekly should be realistic, pulled off your 30-day list and all you work on. Don't worry about your other lists.

At the end of the week, reflect on what you accomplished. If you did not finish your task, ask yourself and accountability partners what you could do different and pull the next most important ones from your 30-day list.

Again, this is just an overview in the coaching process. We do a step-by- step process, but if you are doing it on your own you will follow the overview and fill in with what works best for you.

But through the process, no matter what it is, ask yourself "Is my purposed aligned?"
"How will this benefit others?"
"Is it client focused?"
"Do I have creative solutions?"

If starting a small business, addressing family or organization changes, you should have the process started, from concept to completion, in 6-8 weeks. If not, you have to evaluate and self-reflect on many things.

Romans 8:28-29
28 And we know that in all things God works for the good of those who love him, who have been

called according to his purpose. 29 For those God foreknew, he also predestined to be conformed to the image of his Son, that he might be the firstborn among many brothers and sisters.

[the good... that which conforms us "to the image of his Son" Effectual calling: the call of God to which there is invariably a positive response. Foreknew... some insist that the knowledge here is not abstract, but is couched in love and mixed with purpose. They hold that God not only knew us before we had any knowledge of him, but that he also knew us in the sense of choosing us by his grace, before the foundation of the world. Others believe that Paul here refers to the fact that in eternity past God knew those, who by faith, would become his people. Predestination here is moral conformity to the likeness of his Son. The reason God foreknew, predestined and conformed believers to Christ's likeness is that the Son might hold the position of highest honor in the great family of God.]

Let me again please ask. Do you feel a calling toward it? If not, I am not saying you cannot have worldly success, but it won't be your encompassed path.

And if you will not put in the work, you will not have the results. You need to take every part of this - every topic, every thought, get the knowledge, if you do not have it, and take control of your life. Then you will have the life you deserve.

If you chose to put this book down and sit on the couch and binge watch television, you will get that life.

If you decide to take action and start on achieving an encompassed life, you will get the life you have been seeking.

It goes back to cause and effect, and you have the tools, or can get the tools now, to do whatever you desire. So your life from this point forward is exactly what you want it to be and exactly what you have chosen.

I hope you choose wisely, and I hope you get started today.

Conclusion

This book could have been several hundred pages in length, but it was purposefully kept to less than 120 pages so it could be a quick read and inspire action. The book, without acting on it, is just a book. It's time to go do the life-changing actions.

Afterword

The concept behind this book is not to sell copies. Rather, it is to help people and to give a broader scope of how to really make a difference. This meant including some hard subjects, to facilitate real change. This is a quick read, and there are guides coming out to take you step by step through your journey.

Bibliography and Reference List

Cited work from the NIV Bible.

About the Author

You can see more about Bradley Berg at http://Encompassedpurpose.com or https://www.facebook.com/EncompassedPurpose.

Keep up to date on items coming out such as the

in-depth training guides, videos, classes and series.